Heart of the Jungle

The Author

K. K. Gurung was born in 1955 in the Nepal Himalaya and was educated in India, where he studied biology and history. He started work at Tiger Tops Jungle Lodge in Royal Chitwan National Park as a naturalist in 1977. He became Manager of Wildlife in 1979, and is now Manager of the Lodge and its two camps.

Heart of the Jungle

The Wildlife of Chitwan, Nepal

K. K. Gurung

With drawings by the author

ANDRE DEUTSCH
TIGER TOPS

First published 1983 by
André Deutsch Limited
105 Great Russell Street London WC1
in association with Tiger Tops PVT
Limited PO Box 242 Kathmandu Nepal

Typeset by Pioneer, East Sussex
Printed in Hong Kong

ISBN 0 233 97595 0

Contents

Contents

ACKNOWLEDGEMENTS

I wish to express my gratitude to the following:

Dr Charles McDougal gave expert advice and guidance and provided most of the photographs. The photographs of the jungle cat and the sambar were contributed by his wife Margie McDougal. Dr R. L. Fleming (Jr) read through the initial draft of my manuscript and gave valuable suggestions, especially on the birds. Dr H. R. Mishra read the final draft of my manuscript and gave valuable criticisms, comments and advice. Former Senior Warden Mr T. M. Maskey and Warden Ramprit Yadav gave stimulating ideas about the park's problems and management and about the gharial project. Mr B. N. Upreti, Director General of the Department of National Parks and Wildlife Conservation, encouraged me in my work, and various other members of the Department helped me from time to time. Mr B. Khanal, Lecturer at the National History Museum in Kathmandu, checked and corrected the butterfly list. Dr A. Laurie allowed me to use his plant list of Chitwan.

Jim Edwards, Executive Chairman of Tiger Tops Mountain Travel International, showed considerable interest and enthusiasm in my book and offered to act as joint publisher. John Edwards, Managing Director, Tiger Tops, allowed me company facilities for my use. Lisa Van Gruisen, Director of Public Relations, Tiger Tops Mountain Travel International, with her usual efficiency liased between me and my publishers in London. André Deutsch, publisher, greatly encouraged me to write this book and to draw the illustrations.

I have benefited from the knowledge and understanding of different aspects of Chitwan's natural history of my fellow naturalists at Tiger Tops Jungle Lodge: Hashim Tyabji, Gyamtscho Wangdi, Balaram Thapa (who also provided the photographs of the gharials and fishing by locals), Devendra Basnet, Yam Gurung and Man Vijay Singh. Kaluram Tamang and *shikari* Dhan Bahadur

Tamang collected tracings of many mammal tracks. Former and present colleagues Philippa Bibby, Venetia Holliday, Prem Rai, Devika Subba, Iona Sale and Nick Deacock assisted me in many different ways.

For my parents

1 The background

From the vantage-point known as Black Rock, high on the northern flank of the Someshwar Hills, you can look out over one of the loveliest landscapes on earth. Directly below lies the lush valley of Chitwan, traditional stronghold of the rhino and the tiger. Once the whole, broad plain was covered by jungle, but now the forest has been pushed back to the near bank of the Rapti river, which runs from east to west across the middle of the foreground. Beyond it the chequer-board pattern of farm fields stretches away to the north, with patches of mustard standing out brilliant yellow among the greens and browns.

Beyond the farmland, in the middle distance, looms the dark bulk of the Mahabharat Lekh, a range of mountains rising to more than 8,000 feet. Yet even these hills, substantial as they are, are dwarfed by the peaks that spear the sky behind them — for the entire northern horizon, 80 or 90 miles off, is made up of snow summits in dazzling array. From Dhaulagiri in the west, past Annapurna, Macchapuchare, Gangapurna, Manaslu, Himalchuli and Ganesh Himal to Shisha Pangma far in the east, the Himalayan giants gleam like mighty teeth against the deep blue sky, a continuous reminder that the human spectator is looking directly from a tropical environment into an arctic one.

The name 'Chitwan' has several possible meanings, but the one I should like to use for the purpose of this book is the most literal translation of the two Nepali words that make it up: *chit* or *chita* (heart) and *wan* or *ban* (jungle). Chitwan* is thus 'the heart of the jungle', and by a combination of luck and good management the meaning still holds good. The majority of Nepal's forests have been

---

*The name is also spelt Chitawan, but for this book I have used the version that gives the nearest phonetic equivalent.

destroyed by human exploitation, but this one area has been miraculously preserved for posterity.

'Chitwan!' wrote E. A. Smythies, a forest adviser to the Nepalese Government, forty years ago. 'The famous big-game reserve of Nepal, and one of the most beautiful places in the world. Chitwan! An area of mystery and romance, known by repute to many white men, but seen by so few . . .'

The writer's enthusiasm was well founded, for Chitwan was indeed a magical place, long famous for the greatest variety and abundance of wildlife of any area in Asia. Yet it also had the reputation of harbouring a deadly form of malaria, and human life was traditionally short. Fear of contacting the disease kept the hill people above the level of the swamps and stagnant water in which the mosquitoes bred, and the only humans who survived in the valley were the Tharus, an aboriginal tribe who lived in small clearings in the jungle and who, over hundreds of years, had apparently developed some natural resistance to malaria.

At the beginning of the nineteenth century, cultivation in the valley was deliberately prohibited by the Government of Nepal in order to maintain a barrier of disease-ridden forests as a defence against invasion from the south. Then for the century between 1846 and 1950, when the Rana prime ministers were *de facto* rulers of Nepal, Chitwan was declared a private hunting reserve, maintained exclusively for the privileged classes. Penalties for poaching were severe — capital punishment was awarded for killing rhino — and the wildlife in the area thus received a measure of protection.

From time to time great hunts for tiger and rhino were held during the cool, mosquito-free winter months from December to February. The Ranas invited royalty from Europe and the Princely States of India, as well as other foreign dignitaries, to take part in these grand manoeuvres, which were organised on a magnificent scale, often with several hundred elephants being marshalled to round up the game.

For the visit of King George V of England in 1911 no fewer than 600 elephants were assembled from various parts of Nepal. All had to make their way to Chitwan on foot, and for some the journey took several weeks. The Rana Maharajah's elaborate preparations — which included the building of new roads and the construction of a special camp for the King at Kasara — were rewarded with a record bag of 39 tigers, 18 rhino, 4 bears and several leopards, all shot in the space of eleven days.

At the start of such an operation buffalo calves were staked out at selected sites in the jungle, and if a tiger killed one of them, that whole area would be encircled by a ring of closely-packed elephants, with a wall of white cloth erected in front of them. When all was ready, the riflemen, also mounted on elephants, entered the enclosure to despatch the tigers and other big game trapped within. Excitement no doubt ran high, since although a tiger had no chance of eventual escape, it could always hide in the grass and disappear temporarily.

For smaller hunts, different tactics were employed, with perhaps only a dozen elephants. Assuming that the tiger was somewhere near the bait it had killed, two long barriers of white cloth were put up so as to form a funnel, at the narrow end of which the marksman took position on a *machan,* or tree-platform. The elephants, closing in from the wide end of the funnel, would then drive the tiger towards him, and he would have the chance of shooting it at close range. (A modification of this system is used in today's darting operations: the tiger is driven in the same way, but instead of a bullet the gun fires a syringe filled with immobilising drugs.)

Another distinguished visitor to Chitwan was the Prince of Wales, who came in 1921, and during the 1930s three major hunts were held in the valley. The third, staged in 1938-9, in which Lord Linlithgow, the Viceroy of India, took part, broke all previous records with a bag of 120 tigers, 38 rhinos, 27 leopards and 15 bears from Chitwan valley and the surrounding areas. Naturally, after slaughter on such a scale, it took the animals several years to restore their numbers; but since the hunts were held irregularly, and in different areas, their populations gradually recovered. The main secret of their survival was the fact that their habitat remained unharmed; until the end of the 1940s Chitwan contained more than 1,000 square miles of virgin forests, swamps and grasslands, and the abundant fauna included wild elephant, swamp deer and water buffalo.

But then, in 1950, everything began to change. A popular revolt brought about the collapse of the Rana régime, and with it the end of the big hunts. In the hills the economic situation had been deteriorating for several decades. The population grew so fast that people ran out of land on which to grow crops. In desperation they began to cut down the mountain forests for firewood and cattle fodder. With no vegetation to bind the earth on steep gradients, erosion became a severe problem: precious topsoil was blown away by the high winds and washed down into the rivers by the monsoons.

When the land-hungry farmers began to venture down into the plains, the new government felt obliged to open Chitwan for settlement. An agricultural development programme was started, and thousands of hill people poured into the valley in search of land. A malaria-eradication scheme, launched by the Government and the United States Agency for International Development (USAID) in 1954, proved so successful that the whole district was declared malaria-free in 1960.

All this was progress of a kind. But the human influx was so vast and so rapid that inevitably it had a disastrous effect on the wildlife habitat. According to estimates made by the United States Agency for International Development, the population rose from 36,000 in 1950 to 100,000 only ten years later, and by the early 1960s nearly two-thirds of Chitwan's forests had been lost for ever to the encroachment of the human tide.

Poaching became rampant, and little was done to control it. The main target was the rhino, whose horn — renowned for its alleged medicinal properties — already commanded enormous prices in the drugstores of the East.

A force of armed guards, 130 strong, called 'Gaida Gasti', or the 'Rhino Patrol', was recruited from the Forest Territorial Service and mounted patrols from a chain of outposts. Clashes took place between the guards and the intruders, and casualties were suffered on both sides, but the raids continued. Many of the poachers were hill people from the north who shot rhinos with primitive muzzle-loaders or dug pitfalls to trap them, sometimes chopping off the horn of the animal while it was still alive, and leaving it to die of starvation. Other bands of marauders came in from India.

By the end of the 1950s it was clear that if such a decline continued, the rhino and other animals would soon face extinction. Already the swamp deer and the water buffalo had almost disappeared from Chitwan. Therefore, in 1959, the Fauna Preservation Society appointed the distinguished British naturalist E. P. Gee to make a survey. Gee, who had spent most of his life in India and was an authority on its wildlife, recommended the creation of a national park north of the Rapti river, and this was duly established in 1961-2. He also proposed a wildlife sanctuary to the south of the river for a trial period of ten years. After he had surveyed Chitwan again in 1963, this time for both the Fauna Preservation Society and the International Union for the Conservation of Nature, he recommended an extension of the national park to include areas of rhino country still extant in the south.

By then, however, numerous settlements had sprung up within the park and the sanctuary. It was obvious that if the animals were to re-establish themselves, the humans would have to go. In 1963 a government committee investigated the legal status of immigrants in Chitwan; the Land Settlement Commission of 1964 physically removed 22,000 people, including 4,000 from inside the rhino sanctuary, and resettled them elsewhere in the valley — a huge upheaval that caused a great deal of resentment locally.

Drastic though it was, the operation brought little immediate improvement, for the people who had been evicted poured back into the area to collect firewood and fodder; the habitat deteriorated still further, and the rhino population continued to decline. A survey carried out in June 1968 by G. J. Caughley and H. R. Mishra estimated that only a total of between eighty-one and 108 were left. Their report, published in 1969, predicted that unless total protection were afforded, the rhino would disappear by 1980.

In December 1970, therefore, His late Majesty King Mahendra approved the establishment of the national park south of the Rapti river. The boundaries were delineated in March and April of 1971, and preliminary development began in October that year. Royal Chitwan National Park was officially gazetted in 1973 by His Majesty King Birendra and became the first national park in Nepal.

Topography

At the time of its establishment the park covered 210 square miles. After an extension in 1978-9, it now covers 360 square miles, and another enlargement, now proposed, will extend it to 500. As can be seen from a glance at the map on pages 6-7, its shape is extremely

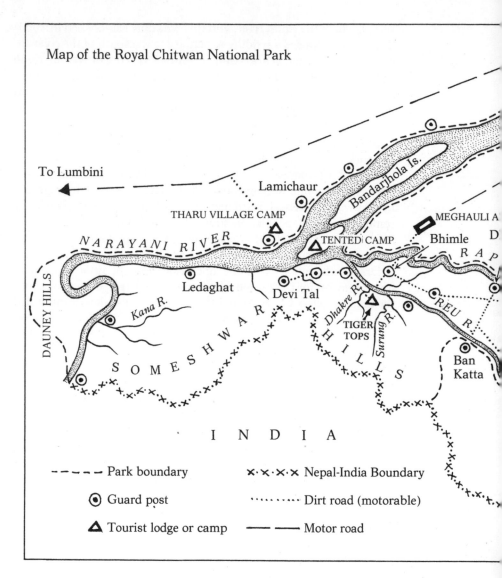

Map of the Royal Chitwan National Park

To Lumbini

Lamichaur

THARU VILLAGE CAMP

Bandarjhola Is.

MEGHAULI A

Bhimle

D

R A P

TENTED CAMP

N A R A Y A N I   R I V E R

Ledaghat

Devi Tal

Dhakre R.

Surung R.

TIGER TOPS

R E U   R.

Kana R.

DAUNEY HILLS

S O M E S H W A R   H I L L S

Ban Katta

I N D I A

- - - - - Park boundary   ×·×·×·× Nepal-India Boundary

⊙ Guard post   ·········· Dirt road (motorable)

△ Tourist lodge or camp   ——— Motor road

irregular and impractical, but this was dictated largely by the disposition of the three rivers which form much of the boundary — the Narayani and the Rapti in the north, and the Reu in the south. More important than the park's shape is the fact that it contains a

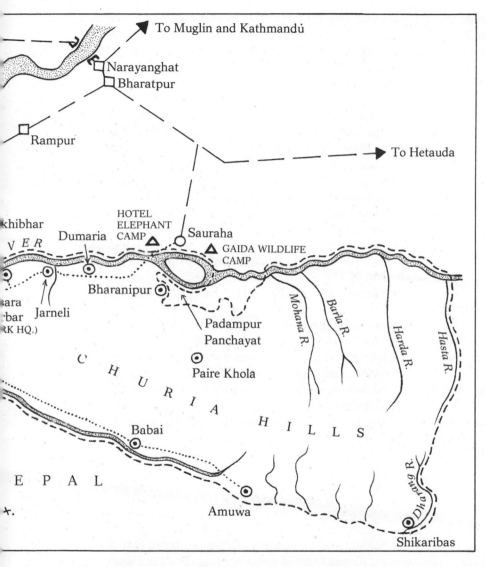

wide variety of habitats, from the grassland and riverine forests of the valleys to the sal forest on the hills and the chir pine that grows along the ridges.

Chitwan is often referred to incorrectly as part of the Terai, the immense flat plain that forms much of the southern edge of Nepal and the northern edge of India. In fact, Chitwan is separated from the Terai first by the Bhabhar, a belt of gently-sloping gravel up to 6 miles wide, and then by the Siwaliks — a line of forested hills which run east and west, rising here to 2,500 feet. A better name for Chitwan is *bhitri madesh*, or Inner Terai. Although only just over 1 mile wide in the east, the valley broadens out to a width of more than 12 miles in the west, and its average elevation is 475 feet above sea level. The broad, flat interior valleys are known as *duns*.

Newcomers to the area are sometimes confused by the fact that many of the local geographical features have several different names. For example the Narayani, which has its origin on the Tibetan plateau and is the third largest river in Nepal, is the same as the Kali Gandaki (the name by which its Himalayan section is known), and after it has flowed out through a narrow gorge near the Indian border, it emerges into Bihar as the Gandak. Similarly, the hills that flank the south side of the Chitwan valley, though part of the Siwalik range, are known as the Churia, the Someshwar and the Dauney Hills.

It should perhaps be emphasised that only a very small part of the park is used for tourism. The great majority of the land, particularly in the hills, remains unvisited and therefore undisturbed. This is ideal for wildlife, and also preserves an element of mystery for humans: because large areas are still unexplored, our knowledge of what birds and animals the park contains is by no means finalised, and there is always the possibility of making new discoveries.

Organisation

The park has its headquarters at Kasara Durbar, 12 miles east of Tiger Tops, where a former hunting lodge once used by the Ranas now contains offices and a small museum. At first the park was patrolled by a force of eighty guards of the Forest Territorial Service, but these have since been replaced by military personnel of the Royal Nepal Army. By 1981, five hundred armed infantry troops guarded the park from twenty-four outposts (it is planned to increase the number of outposts to thirty-two). For effective protection, the park is divided into three administrative districts, with sub-headquarters at Lamichaur (outside the park) in the west, Kasara Durbar in the centre, and Amuwa in the east. Each district is under a commander with the rank of major, who in turn is responsible to the Commanding Officer (a lieutenant-colonel) of the battalion stationed at Bharatpur. Outside the park protection of animals still falls under the jurisdiction of the Rhino Patrol, with its headquarters at Tikoli.

The park is now administered by the Department of National Parks and Wildlife Conservation, a wing of the Ministry of Forests and Soil Conservation. Known until 1980 as the National Parks and Wildlife Conservation Office (NPWCO), this wing was recently elevated to the status of a fully-fledged department. While the local Commanding Officer is responsible for controlling illegal human activities within the park, the Senior Warden is the national park's chief officer. Considerable progress has been made in developing the infrastructure for park management and in controlling poaching and encroachment. In fact, the campaign against poaching has been so successful that not a single case has been recorded within the park since 1976, and there is no doubt that the army constitutes an effective deterrent. The poachers are much more frightened of regular soldiers than of the Rhino Patrol — and with good reason: the military patrol the border with loaded rifles, on foot and by elephant, and if they see a poacher they are allowed in some circumstances to shoot him on sight.

The park itself is funded by the Nepalese Government, but many overseas organisations have shown great generosity in supporting it with money and practical assistance. Funds have been received from the United Nations Development Programme, the Food and Agriculture Organisation, the Fauna Preservation Society (now the Fauna and Flora Preservation Society), the International Union for the Conservation of Nature and Natural Resources, the World Wildlife Fund, and others. In 1973 the Smithsonian Institute and the World Wildlife Fund started the Nepal Tiger Ecology Project based at Sauraha, and in 1978-9 the Frankfurt Zoological Society provided funds for the park extension, as well as for starting a gharial hatching and rearing centre at Kasara.

Climate

Chitwan has a tropical monsoon climate, with high humidity all through the year, and three main seasons.

1. Summer

March to early June are the traditional hot months, with temperatures rising progressively to a peak in May. The highest temperature recorded at this time of year in 1979 at Tiger Tops was 110°F in the shade. In the more open areas, such as the broad sandbanks of the Narayani, mid-afternoon air temperatures sometimes exceed 120°F.

April is peculiar, in that despite the heat of the day the nights can be quite cold. Dust from the plains hangs in the air, and the snow-covered Himalayan peaks are obscured from view for most of the time. Seen through the summer haze, with dust in the air diffusing the light, sunrise and sunset are among Chitwan's most spectacular sights. Dawn is very peaceful. The sun comes up like a giant balloon and seems to hang low over the plain before diminishing to its ordinary size as it climbs. In the evening the sky darkens to deeper and deeper red, with the jungle silhouetted in black against it.

South-westerly winds prevail, and relative humidity is lowest in March. April and May are characterised by sudden, violent thunderstorms carrying sand and hailstones, and high-velocity winds uproot large trees. Severe hailstorms can do considerable damage to crops, houses and property, although the size of the hailstones is almost always exaggerated. Sometimes giant dust storms sweep over the valley, darkening the sky dramatically in the late afternoon.

2. The Monsoon

Towards the end of May the pre-monsoon storms set in. Dark clouds mass in the afternoons, with thunder and lightning and high winds which do much damage to trees. If rain falls, it comes in late-afternoon showers lasting perhaps only fifteen or twenty minutes. As May changes into June the showers come with increasing frequency. In 1981 the pre-monsoon rainfall amounted to nearly 14 inches, but this was an exceptional amount — the highest recorded for years — and normally the precipitation has little effect on the level of the rivers.

When the monsoon proper begins, around the middle of June, it is another story. From then until late September the moisture-laden south-easterly winds sweeping up from the Bay of Bengal bring heavy rain, and of the annual total of some 80 inches, more than 80 per cent falls in these three months.

Many people believe that the monsoon is an unpleasant time in Chitwan, but I myself find it by far the most interesting season of the year. For me it brings a glimpse of a lost epoch, a vision of the past. The sight of the rivers, swollen and raging, with whole 100-foot trees coming down the current like twigs, produces a sensation of primeval wildness. The very atmosphere seems tense, with millions of insects buzzing, and the vegetation pressing in on you, lush, dark and intensely green all round. The presence of the jungle is much stronger, more overwhelming, the closeness of the animals more easily felt. Man seems more vulnerable, dwarfed as he is by these tremendous forces of nature — the rain driving down, the wind lashing, the sun scorching. Yet, paradoxically, although more strongly challenged by nature, man also comes much closer to it. Anyone with a feeling for nature must get the impact of the monsoon: it comes straight at him in the smell that pervades the air — the rich, damp smell of the earth, the smell of water and greenery, the smell of life.

The sheer violence of the rain can be spectacular. On 16 July 1978, over 12 inches fell in twenty-four hours at Tiger Tops, and on 29 September 1981, 10 inches were recorded within seven hours. So heavy was the rain throughout Nepal that night that the resultant floods were highly destructive. The Narayani rose at a prodigious rate, and most of the Bandarjhola Island remained submerged for up to two days. When the floods subsided, the islands were left covered by a deposit of fine silt.

Precipitation is not normally continuous, and often, in any monsoon month, there are as many dry days as wet ones. Yet all over the park, stream-beds which remain dry for most of the year turn into small rivers, and many natural springs erupt along their courses. All the main rivers burst their banks, and extensive areas of the floodplains become inundated for long periods. Even the *tals* (lakes) and *ghols* (swamps) that remain stagnant in the dry period join up with the rivers and maintain a gentle flow. The Reu, which is only a few feet deep in May, becomes impassable even for elephants. The seasonal changes in the river-courses and the intermittent waterlogging are a regular feature of Chitwan, and help maintain the floodplain vegetation in a constant state of flux. On the whole, drainage within the park is good.

During the monsoon humidity is extremely high, promoting the growth of fungus on almost any object: clothes, food, stationery, the insides of cameras and binoculars, and even human skins. Leather shoes and belts are particularly favoured by fungus of various kinds: if left in a dark corner, a pair of shoes can completely change colour in a few days with the dense, velvety growth of primitive, chlorophyll-lacking plants plastered all over them. Human beings, as much as any other creature or object, are bombarded by fungus spores all the time, and if any patch of skin is dirty and damp, they will start to grow. The remedy is to have a shower or a bath at least once a day.

Few tourists come to Chitwan during the monsoon — not least because it is often impossible, because of the rivers, to reach or leave the park for days on end. Yet this is a marvellous time to go out looking for animals, on foot or on elephant-back. One sweats continuously, and one is frequently wet through by rain, as well as plagued by leeches; but any minor discomforts are banished by the excitement of close contact with nature in this wild, raw state.

3. Winter

Winter lasts from October to the end of February. The northerly winds are cool, coming down from the mountains, and this is the best time of year to see the Great Himalayan Range, the air being particularly clear in November.

January is the coldest month, with temperatures falling almost to freezing-point, especially on days of rain. Occasional frosts are recorded. The mid-winter rain, though limited, is nevertheless highly beneficial to crops such as wheat and mustard. From late November the relative humidity touches 100 per cent in the mornings, and so heavy is the dewfall during December and January nights that newcomers to the park, hearing the drips pouring off the trees in the morning, often mistake it for rain.

A heavy fog generally forms in the night and hangs low over the forest, on some days persisting until 11 a.m. or later. This makes early morning the coldest time of day, and because of the dampness the chill is felt even more. After an especially cold start it is hard to believe that the temperature will rise to 70°F or more in the afternoon.

Rainfall at Tiger Tops (Figures in inches)
T = traces

YEAR	JAN	FEB	MAR	APR	MAY	JUN	JUL	AUG	SEP	OCT	NOV	DEC	TOTAL
1977	0.3	0.3	0.07	3.3	6.3	7.6	22.4	20.5	6.3	3.9	T	T	70.97
1978	0.3	0.7	0.7	3.4	2.3	14.2	29.2	14.4	16.9	1.7	T	0.15	83.95
1979	T	1.1	T	1.1	1.1	10.2	27.5	20.2	4.0	1.9	0.4	1.5	69.0
1980	T	0.4	0.5	T	2.9	13.7	16.6	17.0	7.8	1.2	T	T	60.1
1981	2.3	T	T	2.8	6.6	14.9	30.8	34.5	25.7	T	T	T	117.6

Temperatures recorded at Rampur Agricultural
Station, Chitwan — °Fahrenheit

	J	F	M	A	M	J	J	A	S	O	N	D
Maximum												
10-year average												
1971-80	71.7	76.8	87.9	95.0	94.1	92.3	88.5	90.5	88.1	86.0	71.7	73.5
Minimum	44.6	47.8	53.7	65.1	71.7	73.9	76.6	75.9	73.7	66.7	54.6	46.4
Max. monthly												
1980	75.2	83.1	97.1	105.0	101.12	98.9	95.0	99.6	94.8	95.3	85.1	78.8
Min. monthly												
1980	40.1	41.0	48.2	55.4	66.5	69.8	73.9	73.4	70.5	55.4	48.9	42.8

Geology and Palaeontology

By geological standards, the Himalayas are considered recent: they are believed to have emerged from the Sea of Tethys when the Indian landmass collided with the Asian Angaran Block. This entire process is said to have happened in three main waves of upheavals covering several million years, and the mountain-building activity is not yet complete. The Siwaliks are the outermost foothills of the Himalayas, running along the length of southern Nepal and extending for some distance into northern India.

The bedrock appears unstable and rather loose and consists mainly of sandstones, conglomerates, quartzites, shales and micaceous sandstones. The floodplains are characterised by ascending terraces of alluvial deposits from the north.

The Siwaliks have also revealed rich deposits of prehistoric mammalian fossils. The list is enormous and includes several forms of such exotica as the mastodons and elephants, rhinoceroses and hippos, sabre-toothed tigers, giant wild boars, chimpanzees, orang utang and baboon, and even the *Gigantopithecus*, a hominid. The yeti or abominable snowman of the high Himalayan wildernesses that haunts the minds of the mountain-dwellers and questing people alike may be only a myth, but a similar creature could well have roamed here in the distant past.

2 The environment

To a casual observer the pattern of vegetation in Chitwan probably seems stable. On the low-lying flat land near the rivers, including the large islands in the Narayani, there is a lush growth of short and long grass interspersed with patches of mixed forest. On the hills which rise behind Tiger Tops the forest is more uniform, consisting mainly of stately, straight-trunked sal (*Shorea robusta*), a valuable hardwood. Everything, a visitor might think, has been like this for some time.

Yet the apparent stability is an illusion. Nature is constantly in a state of flux, particularly in a monsoon area of this kind, and one of the rewards of working in the park is that it enables one to observe the process — a kind of continuous, creeping takeover — whereby some species of plants and trees gradually gain supremacy over others.

The patterns of succession are as yet poorly understood, and need further investigation. But there are two factors which influence the vegetation of the park more than any others — water and fire.

Every summer during the monsoon floods the rivers change their routes to a greater or lesser extent, altering the configuration of the floodplains. The floods destroy whole tracts of vegetation at various stages of growth, and the islands and sandbanks which emerge as the waters recede become sites for primary succession. Thus, every year, water wipes part of the slate clean and allows a new start to be made.

The freshly-exposed sandbanks are soon colonised by various species of grass. One of the first to arrive is usually *Saccharum spontaneum*, which can eventually grow to become 20 feet tall. Short, fast-growing grasses, and some creeping types, also invade, together with herbs and shrubs.

Certain trees are quick to take advantage too, particularly shisham (*Dalbergia sissoo*), a hardwood related to rosewood, which colonises the newly-created silt-beds almost as fast as grass. Close behind it comes khair (*Acacia catechu*). Both these pioneering species stabilise the soil and create conditions favourable to other trees such as kapok (*Bombax ceiba*), and thus the foundations of a new forest are laid. As the trees become established, the sun-loving grasses are gradually displaced, and other grasses and shrubs appear to form a dense understorey. Patches of stable soil with exceptionally good drainage may even be taken over by sal.

Yet the speed of succession is strongly influenced by the second great controlling factor in Chitwan: fire. This strikes no less regularly than the monsoons.

Since time immemorial the aboriginal inhabitants of the valley have been burning the grasslands in winter and early spring, partly to ensure themselves a good, fresh growth of *Imperata,* the grass they use for thatching, and partly to harden the taller, cane-like grass reeds which they need for the walls of their houses. In the old

days local people harvested grass and reeds whenever they wanted; now there is a limited season, usually in the first two or three weeks of January, in which the park authorities issue entry-permits to villagers at the nominal cost of 25 paisa — less than two US cents — a head.

So important is the occasion in the lives of the local Tharus that they hold special festivals to mark the beginning and the end of the grass-cutting season. Immense numbers of people take part. In January 1981, 55,000 entry-permits were issued, and thousands more illegal entrants no doubt poured into the park as part of the mass invasion.

To prevent poaching and illegal cutting of firewood, there is a rule that nobody may spend the night in the park. Thus hundreds of small temporary settlements suddenly spring up just outside the boundaries, so that the villagers, especially those who live some distance away, can hoard as much grass and reeds as possible during the period allocated. The Rapti and Narayani rivers become densely crowded with dug-out canoes and boats, which provide continual ferry services from the misty mornings until dusk. According to the Senior Warden of the day, T. M. Maskey, some 7 million rupees' worth of grass and stalks were taken out of the park in 1981.

Having collected what they need, the villagers set fire to the grasslands at random, without much supervision. Because, early in the year, many of the grass stands are still green, the first fires are relatively cool: they spread slowly, and are generally put out by the dewfall of winter nights. The numerous water-courses, open banks and artificially-prepared clearings which act as fire-breaks all help contain them.

By March and April, however, the grass is much drier, and now the fires spread much more quickly, fanned by the afternoon winds to such an extent that some areas are burned two or three times over. The flames spread into the riverine forests, and many young trees are destroyed: often the fresh young foliage of the shisham trees is totally charred.

The loud, crackling roar can be heard from a considerable distance as the flames tear through the desiccated grass and other vegetation, laying everything waste. Drongos follow the fires, often dangerously close, manoeuvring with amazing agility to catch the insects that fly off to escape the flames; hen harriers and other raptors hunt for rodents and lizards over the newly-open, burned-out ground.

Now fires climb into the sal forest as well. After the heavy leaf-fall during April, the forest floor is carpeted with a thick layer of dead leaves and twigs: the flames gain a hold in it, and the fires ascend the hills. Often the Siwaliks are still burning at the end of April or the beginning of May. Only in years of heavy pre-monsoon rains, such as 1981, do the sal and other hill forests escape extensive burning.

On the plains, where the water-table is high, the grass soon grows again. New shoots appear within ten or fifteen days of the burning, and although the rate of growth is not high early in the year, it is greatly accelerated by the occasional rains of April and May. By the time the monsoon has set in around mid-June, the new grasses are already 10 feet tall.

The key question, now being much debated, is whether the burning does more good than harm.

Fire appears to be integral to the ecology of Chitwan, and is not a recent factor. Just how long the aboriginal people have been burning grasslands here is not known, but they could well have done it for hundreds of years. Nor are natural fires, started by lightning, by any means an impossibility.

If the grasslands were left unburned, the thick, matted stalks would inhibit new growth and create conditions suitable for trees to establish themselves. Burning is a traditional practice used to perpetuate grasslands and discourage trees from moving in. In the park, the natural plant succession is from grassland to forest, and burning does seem to retard this process — even to reverse it if the fires are severe. It has also been established that grassland and riverine forest produce a greater animal biomass than the monotypic sal forest. Without fire to retard woody invasion, large grassland areas would very likely be taken over by forests, except on the low-lying floodplains; wildlife populations, especially of ungulates and therefore of predators, would be likely to decline not only in numbers but also in quality.

The tall, coarse grasses have little food value once they have grown past the young, palatable stage. By the time they have flowered and are dying, most of their food has been transferred to their roots for storage — an evolutionary adaptation designed to cope with the oncoming dry season. From the animals' point of view, the main importance of dead or dying grass appears to be that it affords cover and shelter; but regrowth is so fast that this factor is regained in a few months after burning. Moreover, not all grass is burnt simultaneously, and animals can and do seek refuge in the sal forest and other areas.

All these factors indicate that, as far as the large mammals are concerned, the grassland-burning is an ecologically-sound exercise. It not only renders the grass edible for more months of the year, but also provides a period of maximum protein/fibre ratio. The herbivores readily move into recently-burned patches to feed on the succulent and nutritious new shoots. The existing mosaic of vegetation is, in part, a result of the fires, and it offers a variety of vegetation types that meets the food requirements of most ungulates.

It may nevertheless be argued that annual burning (especially as it lasts on and off for three months) destroys potential food in the form of edible, standing grasses that would otherwise have been more fully used. Also, repeated burning may be uneconomic, in that it makes excessive demands on the energy stored in the roots of grasses, which have to regrow from scratch every year. In time, only those grasses that are resistant to fire will remain, and the other, less-tolerant species will go. Thus the whole composition and pattern of the grasslands will be altered. This may perhaps explain why most of the short-grass areas have already been displaced by the hardy and aggressive tall, coarse grasses (although other causes, such as the lack of grazing pressure, may have contributed towards this change). It appears that fires do keep trees away, but may also favour tall grasses at the expense of short ones. In the long term all this may affect individual herbivores differently, favouring some and depriving others.

The effects of fire on soil microflora and nutrients, and on other small animals such as birds, reptiles and invertebrates, are not yet known. In so far as they maintain grassland habitats for wildlife, fires serve their purpose well, but overburning without management may be having injurious long-term effects on Chitwan's ecosystem.

Ecologists and park managers are therefore faced with the dilemma of fire or no fire. Should it be every year or every few years? And what is the optimal extent? These are some of the many questions for which answers must soon be found through scientific research if the park is to be managed successfully. Fire, judiciously applied, in conjunction with other means such as physically clearing large areas of the floodplains to create suitable habitats for ungulates, could well be used as a management tool to maintain the park's ecological integrity.

The environment produced by these various factors contains three different elements: the grasslands, the riverine forest and the sal forest.

1. Grasslands

The alluvial floodplains, which occupy about one-fifth of the park's area, support a luxuriant growth of grasses interspersed with patches of riverine forest. All tall, dense stands are popularly called 'elephant grass', and indeed elephants not only eat the stalks but are the best means of transport in such country, where the cover can easily be 20 feet high. At first glance the grassland appears a monotonous type of habitat, yet it contains over fifty species, some only a foot tall. The grassland communities were recorded and mapped in detail by Andrew Laurie in connection with his research on rhinos conducted in Chitwan between 1973 and 1976.

The most important grass, in human terms, is khar (*Imperata cylindrica*), which is vital to the local population for thatching. This can grow up to 7 feet tall, although it usually remains shorter; it dominates on old village sites, especially in areas where the villagers still harvest it. But it has been observed that over the years *Imperata* is steadily giving way to taller and more aggressive species such as *Saccharum*. Before the evacuation of 1964 large areas surrounding the villages were under cultivation, and the grasslands were cut and burned to obtain building materials and to improve grazing for livestock. Pressure from grazing has since been removed from most of these sites, and there is no cultivation. These factors are perhaps partly responsible for *Imperata's* decline.

Other types of grass dominate in different areas, the tallest stands being up to 25 feet high: prominent among these giants are species of *Phragmites, Arundo, Themeda, Narenga* and *Saccharum.* On the whole the shortest grass is to be found along the park's edge, where domestic cattle and buffalo graze illegally within the boundary, usually with the encouragement of their owners.

Most grasses achieve their full growth by the end of the monsoon in September, and maximum flowering takes place from then until November. Although the various stands of each species blossom at the same time wherever they are growing, different species have different peak flowering times, and they present a spectacular sight, with great seas of red, ochre, purple and white waving above the savannah.

The grass communities which have evolved on the plains are highly complex, and the product of many contributing factors. Most of them are not influenced by human interference, except the annual burning.

Yet occasionally there may be a case for drastic corrective action — for instance to curb the spread of water hyacinth (*Eichhornia sp.*). This was introduced into India as an ornamental plant, and indeed when in flower during the summer and the monsoon its purple blossoms make a pleasing contrast with the dark-green vegetation which grows all round the shores of the *tals.* But the water hyacinth has spread so rapidly as to become a menace: by covering the entire surface of lakes, it cuts out the light, kills the fish, and suppresses other forms of plant and animal life. If the species is allowed to grow unchecked, the ecology of the lakes will be seriously upset.

2. Riverine Forests

Riverine forests grow along water-courses, and their composition varies greatly from place to place. On recently-formed alluvial banks, and on large gravel islands such as those of Bandarjhola and Majurtika in the Narayani, the forest is often composed of shisham and khair: the first dominates on moist ground, but the second in drier areas; khair, unlike shisham, can grow well away from water.

Pure, or 'monotypic', stands of either tree are common; both grow to a height of 50 feet, and are valuable timber. In the rainy season khair puts out pale greenish-yellow, aromatic flowers in cylindrical spikes up to 4 inches long. The medicinally-important *catechu* or *kutch* is derived by boiling bits of its heartwood many times over.

The kapok (or *Bombax* — the silk-cotton tree), which often follows next in succession, is one of the largest trees in the park. One reason for its success is that it is resistant to fire. Young kapok have short, conical spines on their trunks to protect them from browsers, but these die away as the tree grows bigger, and older specimens are characterised by the fluted buttresses which bulk out the base of the trunks, as well as by thick horizontal branches. In favourable areas kapok establishes itself in large monotypic stands, such as those found interspersed with the grassland on the plains east of Bhimle. In winter the trees' bare tops stand out above the rolling, grassy landscape in a bold grey tracery that looks particularly fine against the evening sky. Large *Bombax* are often parasitised by mistletoe.

Another common gregarious tree is the jamun (*Syzygium cuminii*), an evergreen which keeps its dark-green foliage the year round. Jamun grow best in damp ground, and have established several monotypic stands in the park; one is to the west of Devi Tal, where the trees are so closely packed that their crowns intercept almost all the sunlight, and the forest floor carries scarcely any undergrowth. Jamun have deep-purple, edible fruit which ripen in July.

Yet another frequent component of riverine forests is bilar, (*Trewia nudiflora*), which also flourishes especially in moist spots. Its bark — a favourite habitat for various lichens — is usually a mosaic of many pastel colours, dominated by white. Lichen also grows profusely on the thin stems of the curry plant (*Murraya koenigii*), whose small, pointed leaves release a characteristic spicy flavour when crushed.

Also partial to low-lying, waterlogged areas is the flame-of-the-forest, or palash (*Butea monosperma*), another gregarious species of middling height, with a crooked trunk and dark bark. Its trifoliate leaves are said to represent the Hindu Trinity — Brahma, Vishnu and Shiva. In February and March both kapok and flame-of-the-forest come into flower, and the blaze of red blossoms on otherwise naked trees is a memorable sight. No less memorable is the overpowering scent of bhanti (*Clerodendrum viscosum*), an under-storey shrub, whose white blossoms come out in the spring.

One exotic invader is proving as great a menace as the water hyacinth: *Lantana camara,* whose Nepali name *ban maruwa* means 'forest killer', and rightly so, is gradually encroaching into many of the riverine forests. This highly-aggressive and prickly climbing shrub — a native of tropical America — easily out-competes the indigenous species and is becoming established in more and more areas.

Figs of many different kinds grow profusely along the banks of rivers, streams and lakes. Some of them, such as the pipal (*Ficus religiosa*) and the kabhro (*Ficus lacor*), start life as ephiphytes (that is, growing out of another tree, which acts as host), and eventually establish a territorial existence of their own. The young shoots of kabhro which sprout in March are considered a delicacy, and the medicinally-valued pipal is a tree sacred to Hindus and Buddhists alike.

Large tracts of dense, mature riverine forest on the Bandarjhola Island support a rich growth of figs, and thus form a haven for fruit-eating birds such as hornbills. Elephants eat the branches with great relish.

3. Sal and Hill Forests

The climax type of vegetation — the last in the natural succession — is the sal forest which grows on the Siwalik Hills and the adjoining high ground. Sal is a hardwood tree which here averages 100 feet in height; although deciduous, it is never entirely leafless, and in spring it becomes laden with mildly-scented, creamy-white flowers. In May and June winged seeds fall to the ground, which has been cleared by recent fires, and quick germination results from the pre- and early-monsoon showers. Recently the seeds have been commercially exploited for the extraction of edible oil.

The tree itself is of great economic value. Its strong and durable timber is used for building houses and bridges, and for railway sleepers. Sal has been extensively used for wood-carving in

Kathmandu; many old palaces and temples there have sal pillars and beams. The natives prepare disposable plates by stitching several leaves together with bamboo pricks: these biodegradables are commonly used during marriage ceremonies and other festivals to feed the guests.

The annual burning perhaps encourages the predominance of this fire-resistant tree. Sal grows neither on recently-formed alluvium nor on poorly-drained soil (prolonged waterlogging caused by the change in course of the Surung river has killed a small patch of this forest near the river's confluence with the Reu). Sal is highly gregarious, and frequently establishes monotypic stands, with a scant shrub layer beneath. In places where the canopy is unbroken, the forest floor is relatively bare, whereas in areas of discontinuous canopies tall, coarse grass often grows 20 feet high.

A large number of other trees, shrubs, creepers, ferns, flowers and grasses grow among or under the sal, and many of these are valued for their special properties. For instance bhalayo (*Semecarpus anacardium*), which grows on some ridges of the Someshwar Hills, is known as the marker-nut tree, because its fruit yields a dye and a marking-ink. The best dug-out canoes are carved from haldu (*Adina cordifolia*), a large tree found in the lower fringes of the sal forest. The bark of the dudhey (*Holarrhena antidysenterica*) provides — as its name suggests — a cure for dysentery, and the bark of sandan (*Ougenia dalbergoides*) furnishes the natives with fish poison. The fruit of both barro (*Terminalia belerica*) and harro (*Terminalia chebula*) possess many medicinal qualities. Another frequent component of the sal forest is saj or asna (*Terminalia tomentosa*), a large tree readily identified by its light-grey, much-cracked bark which from a distance resembles a crocodile's skin. Another common sight is bhorla (*Bauhinia vahilii*), a robust, fast-growing creeper which often smothers whole tree canopies. Its large, leathery, twin-lobed leaves, sometimes 18 inches across, are used by the Tharus to make hats, which resemble those of the Chinese. The leaves are also used as plates and for wrapping meat in India and Nepal. The fruit of the kusum (*Schleichera trijuga*) is so luscious that villagers enter the park illegally to collect it when it ripens in July. The kusum is one of the most colourful trees in the park: its new leaves, which emerge in March and April, come out bright scarlet before changing gradually to dark green.

The high, dry ridges of the Churia carry an interesting mixture of sal and chir pine (*Pinus roxburghii*). The sal here is considerably shorter, and the taller pines compete with it for predominance. The forest floor is quite bare except for the occasional growth of short grasses, and on the whole the trees do not grow densely.

Numerous streams rise in the hills and zigzag their way down to the plains. Their wet and shady water-courses support narrow strips of evergreen vegetation.

Along the lower fringes of the sal, where it merges into other vegetation types, there is a marked increase in the variety of trees. In such transitional zones it is often impossible to say where one type of forest ends and another begins. But many species are versatile enough to grow in either, regardless of what man likes to call the community of which they form part.

3   Ungulates (Hoofed mammals)

Greater One-horned Rhinoceros (*Rhinoceros unicornis*)
Nepali: gainda

The rhino is not only the largest animal in the park (apart from the wild elephant, which is now rarely seen); it is also, to local people, a sacred creature, the object of great veneration, and the possessor of many magical powers. Its unique reputation derives from the belief that it got its horn from Parvati, consort of the god Shiva.

Almost every part of the rhino's anatomy is coveted for some purpose or other. A rhino-skin bracelet will protect its wearer against evil spirits. Fumigating domestic stock with rhino-bone powder is thought to keep foot-and-mouth and other diseases at bay. Rhino dung is a laxative, and, when mixed with tobacco and smoked, cures coughs. In *Shradda,* the Hindu ritual performed on the day of a person's death, a mixture of water and milk is offered to the gods, and if the libation can be made in a cup of rhino skin or horn, it will be that much more effective in bringing peace to the soul of the departed. Both blood and urine are keenly sought after for medicinal purposes.

Sometimes if a rhino has been injured in a fight, lumps of dried, black blood can be found where it has rested along a trail. People collect the lumps, melt them in water, and administer the solution as a cure for menstrual problems or to stop excessive bleeding after childbirth. Urine is collected with equal enthusiasm as a remedy for asthma, stomach pains and tuberculosis. Sometimes the *phanit,* or elephant driver (equivalent of a *mahout* in India) will jump down from his mount to fill a bottle from a recently-deposited puddle. Other people, finding a patch of wet sand where a rhino has urinated, will rinse out the sand with water and drink the strainings.

Rhino meat — even if stinking and maggot-ridden — is collected

and eaten (for health and vigour) with frenzied relish: once villagers
are authorised by the park authorities to take the remains of an
animal away — usually one that has died of old age or disease —
they pour on to and into the carcass with such a rush that they often
carve up each other as well as the putrefying hulk.

Yet the part which exercises by far the greatest fascination and
commands the greatest price is the rhino's horn. Just as in mediaeval
Asia it was believed that cups carved from rhino horn could detect
poison by causing the drink poured into them to froth, or by
splitting in half, so today the drugstores of the Far East sell rhino-
horn products in smart packs as remedies for numerous ailments.
The Chinese do not — as is popularly believed in the West —
prescribe it as an aphrodisiac. Rather, they use it mainly as a fever-
depressant. Only in India — and particularly in the states of
Gujarat and West Bengal — is it used as a sexual stimulant.

According to Dr E. B. Martin, who published a report in 1981, the Chinese regard the horn of *R. unicornis* as the best, and it is therefore the most expensive, costing up to 17,000 US dollars a kilo. Martin also discovered that between 1969 and 1976 the Yemen Arab Republic imported over 22 tons of horn (the equivalent of 7,800 dead rhino) for making the handles of *jambias,* or traditional daggers. These weapons are owned by almost all Yemeni males of fourteen or over, and the best ones, with elaborately-carved rhino-horn handles, cost up to 13,000 dollars apiece.

It was to meet the demands of Oriental medicine, and to furnish Yemenis with their status symbols, that the rhino was sent hurtling towards extinction. It is estimated that during the 1970s, 90 per cent of the rhinos in Africa were wiped out, and if the present rate of decline is not checked, they will be extinct by 1990. In spite of vigorous control measures, poaching continues throughout east Africa, and the price of horn has reached an all-time high.

Apart from the greater one-horns, the four species that survive, and their populations, are as follows: the black (*Diceros bicornis*) 10,000-20,000, in Africa; the white (*Ceratotherium simum*) 4,000, also in Africa; the Sumatran (*Didermocerus sumatrensis*) 300, in Sumatra; and the Javan (*Rhinoceros sondaicus*) 50, in Java. The one-horned rhino was once widely distributed over the floodplains of the Indus, the Ganges and the Brahmaputra; today, apart from a few which still survive in national parks and wildlife reserves, the world population is thought to number between 1,000 and 1,500, and of these some 350 live in Chitwan.

Although slightly smaller than the African white rhino, the one-horn is immensely solid and formidable. A big male stands 6 feet at the shoulder (females are smaller); this massive creature, with its uniquely folded and thickly armour-plated skin, has a truly prehistoric appearance — and indeed it has changed little in the last million years. Its short legs, ending in three toes, can carry it fast over small distances, and, contrary to popular belief, it is an agile mover, capable of quick turns. Unlike the African and the Sumatran rhinos (which have two horns, one behind the other), this animal has only one horn, which is a cemented mass of hair growing from the skin on top of the snout and separate from the skull. The average length of horn is about 8 inches (although the record size from India is 24 inches), and the average weight between 1 and

2 lbs. The horns of males are normally broader at the base and frequently broken, cracked or split from fighting and age. Both sexes carry about the same sized horns. (Males can be distinguished by their larger neckfolds and a pronounced bib of skin under the chin.)

The role of the horn is obscure. Evolution seldom produces any feature that has no function, so it is reasonable to assume that the horn must serve some purpose. It is not a weapon: although a rhino may strike with it accidentally, the tusks are the real means of attack. It may be that the horn has some ethological function and, by its appearance, announces something about the physical condition of its owner.

Essentially grazers, rhinos also feed on leaves and twigs, aquatic plants and agricultural crops. They seem to obtain their food and other requirements within a fairly small area, and so occupy small home ranges that vary from season to season. They are solitary animals, except when in cow-calf pairs, but they gather near wallows temporarily in summer, and up to twelve have been seen together in a small stretch of the Old Rapti. During the hot months they spend a lot of their time in the water to cool their large bodies. When they come out, and the coating of mud dries, they change colour completely, taking on the light brown or grey of the river bank.

During the breeding season fights between males are frequent, and these are noisy affairs. The large lower tusks are capable of inflicting severe cuts, and some rhinos have been known to die of the wounds sustained in battle. Scars left from such cuts are permanent, and, depending on their position on the body, can be useful as an aid in the identification of individuals.

Males squirt urine backwards, and it is believed that the dominant males eject their urine the furthest. Copulation between rhinos has been observed a few times during spring: the act itself is quite prolonged, often lasting up to an hour. Gestation lasts sixteen to sixteen and a half months and one calf is normally born at a time. At birth the baby is pink and weighs about 150 lbs. The longest association among rhinos is between the mother and her offspring, who stay together for three years or even longer. Young rhinos become sexually mature by the age of ten, and perhaps live fifty years or more.

Very young calves may be taken by tigers, but this happens only rarely, as a tiger finds it hard to beat the mother's vigilance. Although they have no natural enemies, they are most unpredictable by nature and have been known to charge without provocation, perhaps because of their short sight. One old rhino, peacefully feeding, suddenly charged at and knocked down a bicycle parked nearby, with no human anywhere near it. Their bad eyesight is to some extent compensated for by good senses of hearing and smell. When disturbed or surprised they usually bolt 20 or 30 yards, with a loud snort, and then stand still to investigate the cause of their disturbance. They *have* to stand still to find out what is happening, because when they are on the move, particularly through long grass, they make so much noise that they probably cannot hear anything at all.

If approached by humans either on foot or on an elephant, they generally retreat, but females with young can be dangerous, since they stand their ground and are likely to attack. In fact elephants become visibly nervous when close to an agitated cow-calf pair. They can be trained to remain steady in the face of a charging rhino, but whether they will hold their ground depends on the degree of control exercised by the *phanit*. Rhinos usually charge only to veer away at the last moment — a form of threat-display designed to warn off intruders. Very exceptionally, a rhino may press home its charge: once a male elephant belonging to Tiger Tops was badly gashed in the leg by a female who was with her two-year-old calf. After his recovery, which took several months, he became highly aggressive towards *any* rhino. Nowadays, the Chitwan rhinos have become more and more accustomed to seeing elephants with people on them and are showing increasing tolerance towards them.

Nevertheless they are among the most dangerous animals in the park, and they are responsible for a few human deaths and casualties almost every year, particularly during the period when villagers come in to cut grass and reeds: with people swarming in by the thousand, a few inevitably get knocked down and trampled.

It is pleasant to be able to report that conservation of the rhino has been *the* big success story of Chitwan. In 1950, it is thought, there were still about 800 in the valley, but poaching and habitat-destruction sent the population plummeting to its low point of scarcely 100 in the 1960s. Since the establishment of the park, numbers have gradually recovered. During the study which he carried out from 1973 to 1976, the Scottish wildlife biologist Andrew Laurie visually identified about 200 individuals by recording details such as scars, skin-folds and the shape and size of horn, and by 1982 the population was thought to have reached 350.

Rhinos are now so plentiful as to be a positive menace to farmers living around the park boundary. There can be no argument but that they get the best of both worlds. By day they stay in the peaceful sanctuary of the park, and at night they sally forth to feast on the crops in the farmland. Villagers are forced to stay up all night to defend their fields with fire-crackers, torches, javelins and tin-can drums, and in spite of their efforts they suffer severe losses: one survey published in 1980 estimated that between 1975 and 1978 villages in the Padampur *panchayat* near Sauraha suffered 80-90 per cent crop damage from rhino and other wildlife. Nor can the people claim compensation, for the Government feels that any scheme would be open to intolerable abuse: if a crop were eaten in the night, how would the owner prove that the damage had been done by wild animals rather than by his own or his neighbour's cattle, which are never properly under control in any case?

The villagers concerned are beginning to realise that living on the fringe of the park is an occupational hazard which they just have to accept. The wildlife authorities can at least point out that a form of compensation does exist — the villagers' right to collect building material from the forest.

The greatest problem facing the wildlife department on the rhino front is that of what to do with the surplus population if the present annual increase-rate of 2-6 per cent is maintained. To make a scientific cull of old or sick animals is one possibility — but not one that recommends itself to any true animal-lover. A more constructive alternative would be to capture some rhinos live and move them either to zoos or to other parks such as Bardia in far western Nepal and Dudhwa in northern India, where recolonisation projects are already being mooted. The darting and translocation of such large animals is a major undertaking, but it has already been successfully accomplished in Kenya, for instance, and in recent years rhinos darted in Chitwan have been sent to China, Pakistan and Burma.

At present the one-horned rhino exists in strength in only two locations — Chitwan in Nepal and Kaziranga in Assam, India — and if some epidemic were to sweep through either or both of these pockets, the chance of random extinction would be very high. Translocation of rhinos to other suitable areas would greatly increase their chance of ultimate survival.

Gaur *(Bos gaurus) Nepali: gauri gai*

The gaur is the largest form of wild cattle in the world, a magnificent animal of great strength and distinction. Somehow it is much more sophisticated than the primeval rhino: a big bull, with his jet black hide and curving horns, his strong personality and majestic way of moving, looks like a symbol of power and confidence. The sight of one in the early morning, perhaps staring down at the human

intruder from a misty ridge, is one that nobody can soon forget. Six feet tall at the shoulder and weighing close on 2,000 lbs, he can dominate a scene instantly.

The gaur is distributed from the Himalayan foothills and India to the Malay peninsula and Indochina. Calves are born golden yellow, but they darken to reddish brown as they grow up. Young bulls and cows remain this colour, whereas old bulls turn black. Adult gaur have a conspicuous dorsal ridge (larger in males), a dewlap under the chin, thick horns sweeping up from a whitish forehead, and white stockinged feet. The white parts are normally stained yellow, especially in adult bulls, by the slightly aromatic, oily secretion that the body exudes: the purpose of this discharge is not clear, but it seems to play some part in communication.

Gaur are mixed grazers and browsers, and active mainly at night. In the park they mostly inhabit the remote hill forests of the Siwaliks, and for much of the year they are hard to find in that rugged terrain. But during the dry months from January to May, when food and water become scarce in the mountains, they descend to the plains to feed on the luxuriant growth of new grass. In this season herds of ten or twenty are commonly seen around Devi Tal, and solitary bulls are also encountered. When approached by humans on elephants they usually shy away, but on one occasion a cow sheltering a week-old calf stood her ground 10 yards from us and retreated only when her calf was ready to move. In Chitwan gaur herds are usually seen with newborn calves in February and March.

Interbreeding between gaur and domestic cattle occurs in northeast India and northern Burma, and the hybrids are called *gayal* or *mithun*. Unlike the gaur proper, these have straight horns, and they are little valued by local people because they are too big for the plough. Also, they tend to be intractable, and the females give little milk. Being related to the sacred cow, the hybrids have religious protection: because they are useless, and humans may not kill them, they often wander away and go feral.

It seems a pity that the gaur's breeding potential cannot be more profitably exploited. Recently in the Bronx Zoo, New York, a gaur embryo was taken and transplanted into a Holstein cow, which successfully carried to term and bore a male calf. The female gaur was mated again and produced another calf within the same year.

(The oestrus of the gaur and the Holstein cow was synchronised by the use of hormones.)

In the park the gaur seem to be on the decline — not because they are harassed by humans, but because their habitat has shrunk so much. Also, their numbers were drastically reduced by foot-and-mouth disease in the late 1960s. The population — not known for certain — may be between three and four hundred.

Wild Boar *(Sus scrofa) Nepali: Bandel*

A very common animal in the park, the wild boar is found in all habitats but prefers the floodplains. Although larger animals have been recorded from other areas, those found in Chitwan are about 2'6" tall and weigh up to 350 lbs. Adults are nearly black, with coarse hair and a dorsal mane of black bristles: piglets are brownish with dark stripes along their backs. A normal litter consists of from four to twelve, but sounders of ten to fifteen piglets with one or more adults are often seen. During the monsoon larger groups of up to thirty animals have sometimes been found. They are prolific breeders, and the female builds a nest of grass and vegetation before giving birth. The gestation period is about four months. The population may fluctuate wildly, as happened in 1974 when some unknown disease swept through Chitwan. After the epidemic, the density of wild boar was estimated at 12.4 per square mile in the riverine forest and grassland and 6.7 in the sal forest.

Wild boar are omnivorous and feed on roots, tubers, crops, snakes, insects, offal and carrion. They do much damage to crops in the villages, and boars have also been known to attack people. Large boars, with their powerful tusks and incredible speed of movement, are formidable enemies even for a tiger, and they have sometimes inflicted mortal wounds on tigers and leopards — their natural predators — in battles.

The Survival Anglia television film 'The Leopard That Changed Its Spots' contains a memorable sequence, shot in Sri Lanka, in which a leopard is routed and injured by a group of sows defending their young. After an abortive stalk, the leopard turns tail and flees but is actually overtaken and flung into the air by the avenging pigs, which show phenomenal acceleration over a short distance.

At the remains of tiger and leopard kills they are the most voracious scavengers. A fascinating form of competition has been observed at the Tiger Tops leopard blind, or hide, where a big boar has become a serious contender for the live goats staked out as bait to attract leopards. On many occasions, just as the leopard has settled to feed on its kill, the pig has chased it away and taken over the dead animal. Normally the cat regains its prey after the boar has had a feed, but a few times the boar has not even waited for the leopard in the first place: with his razor-sharp tusks he has incapacitated the goat and disembowelled it, ripping great chunks out of it before the poor creature was even dead. This struggle for supremacy has been going on for the past three years.

An interesting story is told of how, in some parts of Nepal, several wild boars can be killed with a single arrow. A hunter, perched on trees, shoots an arrow at the master boar of the group, who, thinking that he has been attacked by others, in a wild frenzy swiftly kills several of them before succumbing himself. According to Hindu mythology, one incarnation of Vishnu was Varaha, the boar.

Sambar *(Cervus unicolor) Nepali: Sambar*

Sambar are big, chunky-looking deer, widely distributed throughout South and South-east Asia. The stags, standing nearly 5 feet at the shoulder and weighing up to 700 lbs, are formidable animals; hinds are a good deal smaller. Both sexes have coarse, grey-brown coats, some much darker than others. Stags grow a distinct, mane-like ruff of hair round their necks, and adult stags carry impressive three-tined antlers.

In Chitwan the sambar are found in all habitats, living in herds up to ten strong, but they prefer the densely-forested hills. They feed mainly at night, and this, coupled with their elusive nature, makes them the hardest to see of all the deer in the park. Largely browsers, they also eat grasses and fruit. When alarmed, they utter an explosive bellow, loud and harsh, generally rendered as *dhank!*, which carries a considerable distance. Like all the other species of deer, they give every possible warning of impending danger, not only calling, but pricking their ears, raising their tails

(both visual signals) and stamping their feet on the ground.

Because of their wide distribution in the park, and their considerable size, they are an important prey species for the tigers. The Nepalese biologist Dr Hemant Mishra, who published a survey of Chitwan's ungulates in 1982, estimated their density in the park at 5.9 per square mile.

At the peak of the rutting season in November and December stags spar with rivals for ownership of a territory — more a form of ritual combat than a real fight — and mate with females entering it. One calf is born after a gestation period of about eight months.

Spotted Deer or Chital *(Axis axis) Nepali: chitri, chital*

Perhaps the most beautiful of all the world's deer, chital are found in Nepal, India and Sri Lanka. Their most distinctive feature is their rich brown coat, strongly spotted in white (the colours being brightest during the monsoon, and fading during the hot, dry period). Large stags reach over 3 feet at the shoulder and weigh up to 200 lbs, hinds about 130 lbs. The stags have graceful, three-tined antlers with the brow tine at right-angles to the main beam. The hinds, with their long, slender necks and legs, are exceptionally elegant.

Chital feed mainly on grass, but supplement their diet with browse and fruit, and also raid cultivated crops. Within the park they shun precipitous terrain, and are found in the grasslands and

the forests wherever water is available. Mishra estimated their density at 54.5 per square mile.

Chital are the most gregarious deer in Chitwan, often being seen in groups of ten to twenty, and sometimes in herds of over a hundred when new grass is shooting from recently-burned areas. The main rutting season seems to be from March to June, when the distinctive bellow of the stags — a loud, rather nasal call — becomes a familiar sound; but fawns appear in all seasons, and so do stags with antlers in velvet.

Because they are less nocturnal than sambar, chital are much easier to see, often feeding in the mornings and afternoons. In the sal forest they commonly follow troops of langurs foraging in the treetops, and clean up the young leaves, fruit, flowers and shoots dropped by the wasteful monkeys.

Their alarm call — an abrupt, piping whistle — generally gives warning of the presence of a leopard or a tiger. Sometimes, if the deer are not sure exactly where the danger lies, the whole forest starts ringing with alarm calls from other chital nearby, and often langurs and peacocks take up the alarm as well.

Much useful information has been collected by H. R. Mishra, a Nepali wildlife biologist who recently completed a three-year research project on the ecology of the chital in Chitwan for his PhD at Edinburgh University.

Hog Deer *(Axis porcinus) Nepali: laguna, para*

The hog deer's thick-set appearance and peculiar gait — they run with their heads down, and not with the springing bounds of other deer — are reminiscent of a pig, and hence perhaps their name. Rather than jump over undergrowth when travelling fast, they tend to crash through it.

They are found in Nepal and Northern India, and their distribution extends to Burma, Thailand and Indochina. They are absent from peninsular India, but are found in Sri Lanka, to which they were introduced by man.

Adults stand over 2 feet at the shoulder and weigh between 75 and 120 lbs. Their brown coats darken in winter — as they do also with age — but most hog deer seen during the monsoon are

conspicuously spotted, although nowhere near so profusely as chital.

In the park their main habitat is the grassland; being predominantly grazers, they favour the short grasslands along the river bank. Mishra estimated their density at 17.2 to the square mile. Usually they live in small herds of two to five, but larger groups are sometimes seen in clearings.

The stags have slender, three-tined antlers rising from bony pedicles, the brow tine making an acute angle with the main beam. The peak of the rut comes during the monsoon, and the hinds give birth to one calf at a time. Hog deer are exceptionally wary — as they have to be to survive the predation of tigers and leopards — and near swamps and lakes they have also to be on the lookout for python, which are capable of catching and eating them.

Hog deer are closely related to chital, and interbreeding between the two species is known to take place. There is some controversy as to the status of the genus *Axis.* Recently Lekagul and McNeely (1977) have placed it under *Cervus,* as was done by Lydekker (1922) and Koopman (1967).

Barking Deer *(Muntiacus muntjak) Nepali: mirga*

Barking deer get their name from their habit of giving loud, sharp, single barks on a variety of occasions, including when they are alarmed. The sound is the only one they utter, apart from a curious rattling which they make (perhaps with their teeth) when running away.

They are the smallest deer in the park, adult males standing 1'8" to 2 feet at the shoulder and weighing from 45-55 lbs. Males have very small antlers, never more than 4 inches long, with short brow tines and straight, unforked beams which grow backwards almost along the line of the head from hairy pedicles, themselves up to 4 inches long. Their coats are bright chestnut and their gait not unlike that of the hog deer — head down and stiff legged.

They are mixed browsers and grazers found in both the sal and the riverine forests, where they come out to feed during the afternoons, singly or in pairs, and very rarely in threes. In 1982 Mishra estimated their density at 9.9 per square mile. During the rut males spar with rivals, apparently using their canine teeth more than their antlers, which are laid back too flat to be much use as a weapon. The females give birth to one calf, or sometimes two, after a six-month pregnancy. As yet little study has been done in Chitwan on barking deer, and more would be useful.

Serow *(Capricornis sumatraensis)*

This strange-looking goat-antelope is found along forested mountains east to Indochina and south to Sumatra. In Chitwan it inhabits the remote ridges of the Siwalik hills, and so is rarely encountered by man. Adult males have a shoulder height of 3 feet or more and weigh over 220 lbs. Their long legs, large ears, thick necks, curved-back horns some 10 inches long, and well-developed facial glands in front of the eyes all contribute to their unmistakeable gawky appearance. Their colour varies greatly from very dark to chestnut brown.

Serow are extremely sure-footed on precipitous terrain, and can negotiate the trunks of horizontal trees. Usually alone, they are also

seen in small groups of two or three. Females generally give birth to one kid, or sometimes two, after seven months' gestation.

Four-horned Antelope *(Tetraceros quadricornis)*
Nepali: Chowka

This animal of the Indian subcontinent prefers hilly jungle terrain, and has only recently been sighted in the eastern parts of the park, along the lower, south-facing slopes of the Churia Hills. Adult males are about the same size as muntjac — some 24 inches at the shoulder — but they lack the muntjac's rich red colour, being brownish-to-tawny above and white below.

The males have two pairs of horns, the front pair only an inch or so long, and the pair behind up to 4 inches. The horns lack the ringed nature so characteristic of true antelopes. Though usually found singly or in pairs, four-horned antelopes are sometimes seen in groups of three to six. One or two young are born after a six-month pregnancy.

Mention should be made here of two ungulates no longer found in Chitwan.

Wild Buffalo *(Bubalus bubalis) Nepali: Arna*

This animal disappeared from Chitwan around 1960. Small populations of wild buffalo are now found in Kosi Tappu in eastern Nepal, and parts of Assam, Orissa, Andhra Pradesh and Madhya Pradesh in India. In Thailand fewer than forty survive in the Uthai Thani Province, but considerable numbers may still occur in Northern Cambodia (Kampuchea).

The *arna* is the largest of all the world's wild buffaloes — a bigger version of the domesticated buffalo and much more powerfully built. Large males may stand 6 feet at the shoulder and weigh a ton. Their slaty-black colour changes to dirty white on the lower half of their legs; their long, strong horns, which are triangular in cross-section, usually curve upwards and outwards into a wide spread, but some animals have semi-circular horns with tips approaching each other at the top.

Tall and short grasslands with swamps and wetlands are their favourite habitat, and they are essentially grazers. They spend a lot of their time wallowing in water, especially in the hot season. They are always liable to raid crops, and wild bulls frequently interbreed with domestic buffalo, producing robust hybrids which are difficult to handle. They have an excellent sense of smell, good hearing and moderate sight.

They usually live in medium-sized herds. Adults are only rarely killed by tigers, but young and calves are occasionally taken. One calf is usually born after a ten-month gestation. In Chitwan many people refer to gaur as *arna,* but in fact the two are by no means the same. The first is a form of cattle, the second a buffalo, and in spite of some superficial physical resemblances, their horns are quite different.

There has been some speculation about the possibility of reintroducing the wild buffalo into Chitwan; but although the idea is superficially attractive, it needs to be handled with caution, for there must have been some ecological reason that made the buffalo disappear in the first place. More study is required before any such plan is attempted.

Swamp Deer *(Cervus duvauceli) Nepali: gonda* or *barasingha*

The swamp deer became extinct in Chitwan in the early 1960s. This deer is endemic to the Indian subcontinent, and two distinct races are recognised: *C.d. duvauceli*, which inhabits the wetlands of northern India from Corbett to Assam, has splayed hooves, whereas *C.d. branderi*, which lives in the Kanha *maidans*, or meadows, in Madhya Pradesh, has compact hooves suitable for hard ground.

In Nepal swamp deer are now found only in the Shuklaphanta and Bardia wildlife reserves. Smaller than the sambar — an adult stag may stand 4'6" at the shoulder and weigh 400 lbs — they are medium-brown, although males, which have manes, tend to be darker. The stags have the most impressive antlers with up to twelve or more points (the Nepali name *barasingha* literally means 'twelve-point antlers').

In Nepal these grazing animals are seldom found away from marshy grasslands. They are highly gregarious and congregate in very large herds. The ecology of the swamp deer in Shuklaphanta was investigated by the American biologist D. Schaaf in the 1970s.

4   Felids (Cats)

The cats are classified according to whether or not they roar. Those that can and do roar (because of the flexible attachment of the larynx) are of the genus *Panthera*, and the others belong to the genera *Felis* and *Neofelis*.

Tiger *(Panthera tigris tigris) Nepali: Bagh*

Of all the animals in Chitwan, it is the tiger that exerts the greatest fascination. To the Nepalis a tiger is the soul of a dissatisfied man, a creature of enormous and sinister power, some of which they can appropriate for themselves if they eat its flesh. Even if they can scrape up a few grains of dried milk from where a nursing tigress has lain, they consider themselves fortunate. To the visitors who pour in from all over the world, the tiger has become a symbol representing the wildlife of Asia: it is this magnificent animal, above all others, that they want to see.

Fifteen years ago tigers were heading fast towards extinction, and in 1969 they entered the IUCN Red Data Book of Endangered Species. Since then, however, a monumental effort on an international scale has enabled them to fight back, at any rate for the time being.

The key event which set the stage for recovery was the launch by the World Wildlife Fund in 1972 of Operation Tiger in Nepal, India, Bhutan and Bangladesh. The respective governments declared their best remaining tiger habitats as reserves; these totalled fourteen at the time, and several more have since been added. In southern Nepal the Royal Chitwan National Park, the Royal Shuklaphanta Wildlife Reserve and the Royal Bardia Wildlife Reserve were made available as part of the worldwide campaign. Then, in 1973, under the auspices of HM Government, the Smithsonian Institute of

Washington, DC, together with the World Wildlife Fund, set up the Nepal Tiger Ecology Project in Chitwan — a 500,000-dollar study of the tiger and its prey, which used the sophisticated technology of radio telemetry for the first time.

As a result of all these efforts, the Bengal tiger has turned the corner. In Chitwan alone there is an estimated population of about thirty-five breeding adults in the park, and every indication suggests that numbers have levelled off at saturation point. No less important, a great deal of vital information has been gathered together about tigers and their behaviour, much of it coming from Chitwan. No one has done more to increase the sum of knowledge than Dr Chuck McDougal, the present Director of Wildlife at Tiger Tops. In thousands of hours of patient observation he has built up a unique store of knowledge and distilled it into his book *The Face of the*

Tiger, which has become an indispensable work of reference. Many of the facts quoted here are taken from it.

Tigers belong to the continent of Asia. According to one theory they originated in Siberia, and, when the ice-ages drove their prey southwards, they followed the herds to lower latitudes, eventually becoming established from the forests round the Caspian Sea to the steaming jungles of South and South-east Asia. Recent palaeontological evidence, however, suggests that the tiger *originated* in South-east Asia.

Whatever the truth, of the eight recognised races, only five survive. Their populations in the wild, in declining order, are: the Royal Bengal tiger (*P.t. tigris*) 2,500-3,000; the Indochinese tiger (*P.t. corbetti*) 2,000; the Sumatran tiger (*P.t. sumatrae*) 600-800; the Siberian tiger (*P.t. altaica*) 300-400; the Chinese tiger (*P.t. amoyensis*) 100. The Javan tiger (*P.t. sondaica*), which was down to three or four animals a few years ago in the Meru-Betiri reserve of Java, is now believed to be extinct. The Caspian tiger (*P.t. virgata*) has probably been extinct for over a decade. The Balinese tiger (*P.t. balica*) disappeared some four decades ago.

As a general rule the tigers of the southern climes are smaller, shorter furred, darker in colour and more closely striped than their northern counterparts. These adaptations may have evolved to help regulate body heat, and also to match the size of the prey that each race hunts.

Not all tigers are normal-coloured. In the past, white tigers have been recorded in the wild, from Central and Eastern India and from the Nepal Terai. They are very large, and have a white coat with dark brown-grey stripes. Their eyes are bluish and nose and lips grey-pink. The last wild white tiger was captured in the former state of Rewa, in Central India, in 1951. By selectively breeding this male with his own offspring, a pure white breed was obtained. All the white tigers found in the major zoos of the world today come from that stock.

White tigers are recessive mutants that may sporadically appear in any normal-coloured population. These are not albinos, which have pink eyes and faintly visible stripes seen only at certain angles of light. The last known albino was shot in the former state of Cooch Behar. Unlike black panthers, which are common, there has been no authentic record of a black tiger.

The Bengal tiger, found in Nepal, India, Bhutan, Bangladesh and the northern parts of Burma, is intermediate in size between the Siberian and the now-extinct Javan. Large Bengal males weigh up to 550 lbs and measure 10 ft from nose to tip of tail. Females weigh up to 360 lbs. Weights fluctuate considerably from day to day, since a hungry animal can engorge itself with flesh nearly one-fifth of its body weight. The largest tiger ever recorded in Nepal weighed 705 lbs and was shot in Chitwan during the late 1930s. Another measured 11 feet in length. Tigers are the largest of all cats: the lions follow a close second.

Primarily inhabitants of thick forests, they have three basic requirements: abundant prey, shade and cover, and water. Chitwan, with all these, is one of the best remaining tiger habitats in the world. The tigers' main prey in the park are chital, sambar, wild boar and hog deer. They hunt alone by stealth and surprise attack, mainly under cover of darkness. They may, however, be active in daytime as well, especially after an unsuccessful hunt, which must be frequent.

They make the fullest use of their kills by remaining near them and feeding off them, often for three or four days on end; sometimes even longer if they are not disturbed. They have prodigious appetites; one large male observed by Dr McDougal ate 77 lbs of meat in a single night. A fully-gorged tiger may then go without food for many days. However, tigers are highly flexible: when a victim is so large that one animal cannot eat it alone, several others may share the kill.

During the day they prefer to lie up in thick cover where they are unlikely to be disturbed. When the summer weather gets uncomfortably hot, they readily take to water to cool off, and are excellent swimmers. One hot day in May a tiger was seen lying half-submerged in water for several hours off the Bandarjhola Island.

In the light-and-shadow of the dense jungle and tall grass which it inhabits, the tiger's camouflage is perfect. Its tawny to orangy-red coat blends amazingly well with its surroundings, and the pattern of black stripes breaks and confuses its outline, making the animal all but invisible even from close range. Tigers can see well in darkness and perhaps — like most nocturnal creatures — have monochromatic vision; and although they may find it hard to see their prey when it freezes, their eyes are nevertheless highly sensitive to any movement. Their hearing is acute and, together with their sight, plays an important part in hunting. They have a moderate but by no means negligible sense of smell: their nostrils are continually picking up information from the scent sprayed by other tigers and animals in the environment.

They occupy specific home ranges, and by gaining familiarity with particular areas they increase their chances of success in hunting. In Chitwan males hold territories of 15-30 square miles, each encompassing and overlapping the smaller ones (between 6 and 10 square miles) of several females. Their sex ratio is estimated at one male: two to four females. Resident tigers continually patrol their territories to defend them against intrusion by others and employ visual, vocal and chemical means to indicate their occupancy. (A tiger cannot afford to defend his territory by physical presence alone.)

If any area ceases to be used for a long period, such as during the monsoon, it is very likely to be appropriated by another tiger. The strongest tigers hold the best territories. One of the Smithsonian radio tigers, no. 105, once held a large territory of nearly 40 square miles between Sauraha and Dhakre, and at one point served no less than eight females. At the beginning of 1979 he had a bloody dispute with a neighbouring resident male, Mahila Bhale, over an oestrous female, and forced the latter to move further westwards.

The size of each territory is probably determined partly by the amount of prey available, although other ecological restraints may be important. There seems also to be some correlation between the total biomass or live weight of prey and the overall number of tigers. The present estimated population of thirty-five breeding adults in Chitwan perhaps represents the optimal carrying capacity of the area. According to Dr McDougal, while the females compete for the best habitats to maintain themselves and to raise their offspring, the males compete for females. By establishing an exclusive territory, a male tiger not only monopolises mating rights with the tigresses in it but also provides them with the stable conditions which they need to raise his offspring.

The Chitwan tigers are now breeding excellently, and the surplus population of young becoming independent from their mothers each year is more than the park can accommodate. Consequently, after growing up in their natal area, most of them are obliged to disperse into adjoining forests to the east, west and the south. Some, however, acquire territories within the park when local vacancies occur as the result of death or debility. Females generally stay in residence longer than males, who remain in charge of one area for a few years only. Nor are territories fixed entities: they change in time and space. The longest association among tigers is between a mother and her cubs, who stay together for up to two years. Adult males and females associate briefly for a week or two during mating and then generally separate, although longer associations lasting several weeks are on record. Tigers call frequently during periods of sexual activity — a deep, booming moan that resounds through the jungle. Their gestation period lasts from 100 to 105 days, and between two and six cubs are normally born in a litter every other year. Female cubs become fully independent at about two years of age, males earlier.

The raising of cubs is entirely a mother's responsibility, and it calls for heavy investment in time and energy. As the cubs grow larger they compete more and more for resources, not only with their mother but also among themselves. Soon after they are two years old, they usually move out, although female cubs may be tolerated more and even accommodated within or near the mother's range. The newly-independent subadults may hang around on the periphery of other tigers' areas until they can find territories of their own; or, as usually happens, they move out of the park. This shows that the tigers, under a given set of ecological conditions, have worked out a land-tenure system whereby the numbers of residents remain more or less constant, any drastic increase in the total population being a temporary build-up of cubs and subadults.

Their territorial behaviour appears to have stronger dictates than just the food supply, since (according to McDougal) the density of tigers near Tiger Tops, where live animal baits are put out daily for nine months of a year and taken with some regularity, is no greater than in other areas of the park where there is no baiting. Also, when a tigress has large, dependent cubs, and energy demands are at least twice as high as they would be if she had no family, she still relies on the same area to support herself and her offspring.

All these facts indicate that tigers cannot be squeezed beyond a certain limit. Indeed, it appears that tigers are geared for scarcity régimes, in which pressure on resources is high — situations which presumably only occur at intervals of several years because of increased breeding success, reduction in prey numbers, or some other cause. Territorial behaviour is thus a spacing mechanism whereby a certain number of tigers successfully maintain themselves without damaging the food base. Tigers regulate their own numbers so that optimal (not maximal) use is made of their resources, which is in the long-term interest of the species.

But tigers have to do many other things besides eating. Another major consideration (as with all animals) is to maintain their genetic input into the population. Females constantly patrol their areas to protect their resources, and profusely spray the boundaries with their scent, both to indicate their presence and periodically to advertise their condition of oestrus to potential mates. A male ranges far over the territories of several females, and besides keeping intruders out by self-advertisement, also checks the reproductive condition of the females in his area, because if he does not, some other male will.

There is some indication that when a new male takes over the range of an old one, he tries to kill any cubs he finds — a behaviour-trait also observed among common langurs and lions. This practice of infanticide, apparently counter-productive, appears to be the product of deep evolutionary instinct. If a tigress's cubs stay with her, she does not come into season again until they are one and a half to two years old, and thus delays a new male's chance of contributing his genes to heredity. On the other hand, by killing cubs that are not related to him, and of little genetic value as far as he is concerned, the male stimulates the female to go through her cycle faster, so that she can bear his own offspring sooner.

If a new male waits for the cubs of some other father to grow to independence, he is wasting a lot of his time, and thereby reducing his own chance of siring offspring. Thus it is in his own best interests to maintain stability in his area, so that the females can bring as many of his cubs as possible to independence. The tenure of males is usually short, because the intense competition with other males leaves them little option except to act fast and, by human standards, foul — but in nature the end justifies the means, and human moral values are not applicable to relationships among animals.

Since the inception of Operation Tiger there has been much

discussion about the minimum number of tigers needed in any one reserve to maintain a healthy genetic pool and prevent inbreeding. At first the minimum was said to be three hundred, but now it has been admitted that this is an impossible target: no single reserve (in Nepal, at any rate) is big enough to hold such a number, and the new estimate suggests that a population of fifty breeding adults may be self-sustaining, particularly if corridors of forest can be maintained between one reserve and another, so that exchanges can take place. Since the Chitwan park is part of a much larger region, and has extensive areas of forest on three sides of it, there is a good chance that the region as a whole now supports the theoretical minimum of fifty.

Far more humans are seen by tigers than vice-versa — and this presents the staff of the park with a problem. People come to see tigers — but their chances of doing so in the daytime are very small. Because the tigers are nocturnal and secretive, and because the park's vegetation is so thick, daylight sightings are rare. Yet it is important that visitors *should* see tigers in the wild, for only a view of this great predator in action can give any idea of what a splendid creature it is, and how infinitely well worth saving. Therefore, to improve people's chances, a carefully-organised programme of baiting is carried out at Tiger Tops.

At two special sites in the jungle a live buffalo calf is staked out every evening, tied to a post with a strong nylon rope. Some 50 yards away is an elaborate hide, or blind, faced with a thatch of long grass to make it look as natural as possible, and approached from the back by a screened path which is kept swept and sanded. As dusk falls two *shikaris* wait in the hide to see if a tiger will come and kill: the moment one does, a man brings word back to the lodge, and parties hurry out to the site.

Nobody who has approached one of the tiger blinds in the dark will forget the experience of walking silently up the path, with green fireflies gliding among the treetops overhead and the jungle absolutely still except for the zing of insects. Some 200 yards short of the hide everyone is required to remove shoes and to walk the rest of the way barefoot. Once everybody is assembled in the blind and stationed at the peepholes, the *shikari* switches on a powerful searchlight and reveals the tiger on the kill: through good binoculars the sight is breathtaking.

Experience has shown that most of the tigers take no notice of the light. Females tend to be more cautious and circumspect, but on the whole, because the tigers do not associate the light with danger, they feed readily with the lamp switched on. Every precaution has been taken to prevent them connecting the light, or indeed the baiting site, with the presence of humans. It is for this reason that cameras are forbidden in the blind, and that there is such strict insistence on everyone keeping quiet. Provided that considerable care is exercised, it is possible to show tigers to a large number of people in the course of the year without disturbing the tigers at all.

Not that the predators are always so elusive — as one group of visitors discovered on their way to the airport. Their elephant was physically halted by a tigress, who appeared out of the long grass in its path, stood up on her hindlegs and roared, and then began to circle in a menacing fashion. For nearly ten minutes the *phanit* was unable to move, and not until he was certain that the tigress had gone away could he bring his elephant on. The four guests on board got the thrill — and the photographic opportunity — of a lifetime. Later investigations showed that the tigress had had her cubs in the area, and the reason for her protective threat-display at once became clear.

A similar instance occurred on the other side of the park, where some of the *shikaris* were out tracking on foot. Suddenly a tigress charged them, roaring, and she landed so close that some of the grass she knocked down brushed against them. When the men went back later on an elephant, they found that, as they suspected, she had given birth to cubs. In yet another case a tigress well known to us as Chuchchi ('Pointed Toes') jumped right on to the head of an elephant which was out foraging for food in the tall grass. She too, it was later discovered, had babies.

If any of these mock attacks had been made on a non-naturalist, it would certainly have been interpreted as an attempt on human life by a man-eater, and a hue-and-cry would probably have been raised. As it was, the reason for the tigresses' aggressive reactions was immediately clear to anybody with training: the mere fact that each of the animals *roared* was in itself proof that their aim was to scare the intruders off, rather than to kill them.

Tiger Study

Apart from the benefit which it confers on visitors, the baiting system is extremely useful for the wildlife staff at Tiger Tops, since it gives them a chance to observe tigers frequently and get to know individuals. Every tiger has distinctive facial and body markings, and with practice it is not difficult to tell one from another. Siblings of the same litter may sometimes have similar facial markings, but even so the stripe patterns on their bodies are usually quite different.

To recognise a tiger by its appearance is one thing; but to study its movements, its range and its dealings with other tigers, one must also be able to recognise its tracks, or pug-marks. By careful investigation of the pug-marks after a known animal has been seen at one of the baiting sites, one can progress, through constant observation, to the stage of being able to identify an individual from its pug-marks alone.

Tigers prefer to travel along river banks or paths made by man or animals, and they inevitably leave a trail of footprints as they go. The marks are larger than life on soft ground, and more realistic on a hard surface. The forefoot makes broad, large and rather square imprints, whereas those of the hindfoot are relatively narrow and long. The tracks of right and left feet slope outwards in the respective directions, and the second toe is set furthest forward. Adult males have larger pug-marks (pad width up to 4 inches) than adult females (pad width up to 3½ inches). Moreover, the toes of females are generally farther separated from the pad than in males and usually — though not always — more pointed.

The tracks of different tigers vary, often considerably, in shape and size, and some animals have giveaway peculiarities such as a claw that does not retract properly or a deformed toe. The tell-tale characteristic may be present in only one foot of a given animal, so the tracks of all its feet must be thoroughly examined. Since tigers are territorial animals, one is likely to encounter only a limited number of tracks in any one area. This minimises the element of confusion, which would be great if one tried to deal with too many at once. Another difficult task is to estimate how *old* pug-marks are;

this, like the whole art of tracking, comes with experience. Dr McDougal has studied the tigers of western Chitwan almost wholly by tracking them with the help of his *shikaris* since 1972.

In 1973 the Nepal Tiger Ecology Project was started in Chitwan. In this important study tigers (also leopards and deer) were darted, tranquillised, fitted with radio collars and then successfully monitored. The main project — directed from Sauraha, on the eastern side of the park — lasted for seven years, ending in 1980, and some additional work was done in 1981. The Smithsonian provided their own equipment, elephants and staff, but personnel from the park naturally joined in some of the operations, and Dr McDougal acted as consultant during the later part of the project. The programme included four major studies, the first two by Americans and the second two by Nepalis:

1. *The movement and activities of tigers* by M. Sunquist
2. *The dispersal pattern among tigers* by J. L. D. Smith
3. *The effects of tiger predation on prey populations* by
   K. M. Tamang
4. *The ecology of the chital (Axis axis)* by H. R. Mishra

The start of each darting expedition very much resembled one of the old-time hunts. Buffalo calves were staked out as bait in the afternoon, along well-known travelled routes in areas with the kind of dense cover into which tigers prefer to drag their kill, and with enough trees from which to fire a dart. If a calf was taken in the night, the tiger's tracks and drag-marks were followed-up early in the morning, the assumption being that it would be with its kill not far away.

Before a drive, several sections of white cloth about 100 feet long were joined end-to-end and erected through the vegetation to form continuous barriers about 5 feet high. Two such barriers were set up so as to make a funnel, at the narrow end of which the person with the tranquilliser gun settled himself in a tree.

Usually four elephants were used to drive the jungle from the mouth of the funnel towards the marksman — a manoeuvre which always caused much noise and disturbance. When a tiger was sighted within shooting range (no more than 20 or 30 yards), a syringe-dart was fired from a Cap-Chur gun at the muscles of the shoulder or the flanks. It was usually possible to see whether or not

the missile had found its mark, for a well-aimed dart would remain hanging from the tiger's skin. In the event of a hit, a few minutes were allowed to pass before any attempt at a follow-up was made.

Since the operation was being carried out in tall grass and forest, where tracking was slow and difficult, the tiger was often temporarily lost, sometimes for as long as an hour. An anaesthetised tiger is highly vulnerable: its body temperature rises as a side-effect of the drug, and physically-weak individuals are particularly at risk in the hot weather — there is a danger of suffocation and even of drowning. (Tiger 105 died thus, falling into a pool as he was presumably trying to drink when not fully conscious.) There was also the possibility of attack from other animals such as a rhino or another tiger, either of which might go for a creature which they saw behaving in an abnormal way.

As a safety measure, a small transmitter was attached to the dart itself, so that a quick follow-up could be made with a radio receiver, but this did not always work. If no transmitter was available, the tracking had to be done by old-fashioned methods. I myself was amazed by the skill with which the professional *shikaris* interpreted the signs, no matter how faint they might be, and distinguished the marks made by the animal they were after from those of others.

If the darted tiger was found not fully unconscious, another dose of tranquilliser was administered before handling. Then care had to be taken that the animal was put in the shade and resting on its side (so as not to put undue pressure on internal organs), with its head supported on a pillow of grass. Sometimes, water had to be poured over it to keep it cool.

The animal was then tattooed on the ear with a number (the first tiger was no. 101, the second 102, and so on), checked for ectoparasites and inspected for general physical condition. Next it was weighed in a cotton sling suspended from a spring balance (no easy job with a 500-lb animal), measured and photographed, so that its size, markings and pad-widths were recorded for future identification. An examination of its canines generally gave some indication of its age. Finally it was fitted with a plastic collar containing a radio transmitter operated by two lithium batteries (with a life of two or three years) and an antenna glued between the two strips of the collar with only a small portion sticking out. The entire radio-collar weighed just over 2 lbs. The tiger regained consciousness in five to seven hours, and was under constant observation throughout that period.

Each transmitter had a different frequency, and radio-tracking was carried out with a battery-operated portable receiver set connected to a hand-held antenna and headphones. The tigers were radio-tracked from aircraft, vehicles, elephants or on foot, and it was found that the strength of signals depended heavily on the topography of the terrain and the intervening vegetation: reception, minimal in the sal forest, improved greatly in open areas. Aerial monitoring was the most effective, but its cost was prohibitive. Elephants and Land Rovers proved the most practical means of transport for tracking operations.

The last tiger in the project, no. 127, was of special interest. After a man had been killed in a particular area, this tiger, a big male, fell under suspicion; but rather than shoot him, the park staff decided to give him the benefit of the doubt and place him under radio surveillance. When darted, he was found to be in excellent condition, yet he killed three more people in the months that followed. Then, for a year, he did not touch humans, and finally he disappeared.

The Smithsonian project as a whole was a great success, although not without its setbacks and bizarre occurrences. Once Kirti Man Tamang, perched in a tree 15 feet off the ground, was brought down by an angry tigress (who had very small babies), but fortunately he survived, with flesh torn from his leg and other injuries. On another occasion Melvin Sunquist, the American scientist tracking tigress 106, was puzzled to find that she seemed to be outside the park in the middle of the day. He became more and more baffled as the radio signals led him towards a village on the far bank of the Narayani, and by the time he reached the village itself he was incredulous. The mystery was solved when he entered one of the huts and found the tigress's collar, still transmitting. Inquiries showed that she had been poisoned, along with a leopard, after she had killed one of villagers' cows, and a man had kept her collar without realising that it was still sending out signals. A similar fate overtook tiger 120, whose collar was also found in a hut, and the remains of tiger 123 were discovered about a month after its death through its radio still transmitting.

Most of the radio-monitoring was done in the daytime, whereas Dr McDougal's study of tracks revealed mainly what had happened at night; but in general the two forms of research proved complementary. No single technique is perfect, but by marrying the two sets of results, it became possible to form a much clearer and more realistic picture of the tigers' social interaction, system of land tenure, and so on.

What all the research has shown, beyond doubt, is that tigers need really large areas if they are to thrive. Science has confirmed what instinct tells one anyway: that the only way to maintain a viable tiger population is to set aside big reserves fully protected from human intrusion, to surround the reserves with large buffer areas, and to link one reserve to the next by means of wide forest corridors.

Leopard *(Panthera pardus) Nepali: Chituwa*

Leopards — also known as panthers, especially in the vocabulary of hunters — are the number two predators in Chitwan, and their activity patterns are much influenced by the dominating presence of the tigers. For instance, they may temporarily move out of an area heavily used by tigers, or become less mobile, or avoid a tiger's main thoroughfares. They also tend to become hyper-cautious and do most of their moving by day, when the tigers are least active. Their secondary status is perfectly illustrated by the example of Sri Lanka: in that environment, where no tigers exist, the leopards occupy the top of the food chain, and so have no other predator to fear. As a result, they are active in broad daylight and hunt even at high noon.

Another factor which encourages leopards in all environments to lead a more diurnal life than tigers is that they are more tolerant of the sun. Furnished as they are with much less massive bodies, they have a higher ratio of skin-area to volume, and so can dissipate heat faster. In daylight their excellent camouflage enables them to blend perfectly with the surroundings, and in stalking prey they can use the barest of cover to deadly advantage. Unlike the tiger they are not exclusively animals of the dense forest, and they have adapted to live in scrub, open country, woodlands and near villages, which makes them the most successful members of the genus *Panthera.*

In Chitwan — unfortunately for visitors — they are extremely elusive, and to increase the frequency of sightings a special baiting site is maintained on the same pattern as those for the tigers, except that a goat is staked out rather than a buffalo calf. Because leopards are less shy than tigers, and often come close to human settlements, the site is only about 300 yards from the lodge.

The leopard is the most widely distributed of all the great cats,

and is found both in Asia and in Africa. Of the dozen subspecies recognised in Asia, the Nepalese leopard is regarded as a distinct race. A big male weighs up to 160 lbs and measures over 8 feet from nose-tip to tail-tip — although 6'6" is more like the average. Females weigh from 90 to 115 lbs. The normal coat colour is fulvous-tawny, and the black markings take the form of rosettes that enclose some of the colour of the background. There are, however, two colour phases — spotted and melanistic, or black — and cubs of both forms may be born in the same litter. The melanistic phase is more common in wet, rainforest areas such as Malaysia, where spotted animals are rare (it has been suggested that the gene for melanism is recessive, with a lower reproductive rate).

Like the tiger, and perhaps even more so, the leopard is a solitary hunter (although a male and female were once seen killing a goat together at the leopard blind). Because of its smaller body size, it goes for smaller animals: chital, hog deer, muntjac, langur, rhesus and porcupine are its main prey. When forced to live in a suboptimal habitat where natural prey is not abundant, such as the marginal areas around the park, it readily subsists on domestic livestock (calves of cattle and buffalo, pigs, goats, sheep), dogs and poultry.

A leopard kill can often be distinguished from that of a tiger by the pattern in which the animal has been eaten. Whereas a tiger starts to feed from the haunches upwards, a leopard usually opens up the belly and the lower chest area.

Unlike in Africa, where leopards habitually take their kills up into the safety of the trees, those in Chitwan do this only occasionally: because of the thick vegetation and limited visibility, they are less likely to be disturbed at their kills by other predators and scavengers than are their counterparts in the open plains of Africa.

Nevertheless, they are wonderful tree-climbers. Unlike tigers, which climb trees when they are subadult, but thereafter become too heavy, leopards can go straight up and down bare tree-trunks, and in general display amazing agility.

Male and female leopards associate briefly during periods of sexual activity, and their rasp-like mating call, known as 'sawing', is unmistakable. Between two and four cubs are born after a gestation period of ninety-five to a hundred days.

Leopard Cat *(Felis bengalensis)*

The leopard cat is the smallest felid in Chitwan, weighing only about 7 to 12 lbs and measuring about 3 feet including the tail, which is always more than one-third of the total body length. The coat is golden yellow, with black and deep-brown spots arranged in

longitudinal rows, the markings being boldest around the shoulders. The leopard cat's distribution extends from Nepal to Java and Kalimantan and north to Amur in the USSR. Because it is nocturnal, and spends much of its time in trees, this predator is rarely seen in the park. Its gestation period is nine or ten weeks and two or three cubs are born at a time.

Jungle Cat *(Felis chaus) Nepali: ban biralo*

About the same length as the leopard cat, but distinguished by its shorter tail and heavier build, the jungle cat is ochre-grey with dark stripes on the thighs and forelegs and a ringed tail tipped with black. It is widely distributed from northern Africa to Indochina. In the park it is found in the grasslands and the fringes of forests, and it is perhaps more diurnal than the other cats, hunting mammals and small birds in daylight. It is said to breed twice a year.

See illustration on page 62.

Jungle Cat

Marbled Cat *(Felis marmorata)*

The colouration and markings of the marbled cat vary so much that it can easily be mistaken for a small clouded leopard (*Neofelis nebulosa*); but the latter is considerably larger (up to 6 feet long overall, as against about 3′6″), and is unlikely to occur in Chitwan.

The marbled cat has dark stripes on its head, neck and back, and

Clouded Leopard

marbled patterns of black-edged blotches (not the large clouds of the clouded leopard) that tend to merge together on its flanks, all against a rich ochre-brown background. Other differences are that the stripes on the cat's head start from the inner side of its eyes, whereas the leopard has a spotted forehead; also the cat has a spotted tail, quite different from the leopard's, which is widely banded towards the end.

The marbled cat's distribution ranges from Nepal through Indochina to Sumatra and Kalimantan. It is an animal of the dense forest and preys on small mammals at night. Its long tail and low body suggest that it is mainly arboreal. A marbled cat was found in the Nawalpur area, to the west of Chitwan, and it is suspected of occurring in the valley.

Fishing Cat *(Felis viverrina)*

This compact-looking cat, with a relatively short tail, occurs patchily from India to Java. Adults weigh 20-35 lbs and measure about 4 feet long including the tail, which is much less than one-third of the total length. The fur is mixed brown-grey with rows of longitudinally-elongated dark spots, which converge as stripes on the top of the neck and the forehead. There are also two horizontal black stripes on the white cheeks.

   Its forefeet have webbed toes, and the claws are not fully retractile. It feeds mainly on fish scooped out of water and other aquatic animals such as molluscs, but in the thick forests and grass swamps which it frequents it also hunts small mammals and birds. The fishing cat may take larger prey and has been known to scavenge on tiger and leopard kills. Two or three cubs are born after a gestation period of three months.

5 Canids, hyenas and bears

Wild Dog *(Cuon alpinus) Nepali: Ban kukur*

An animal of Central, Southern and South-eastern Asia, the *dhole* (its Indian name) is quite different from the African wild dog (*Lycaon pictus*). Whereas the African dog is mottled black and grey-brown, the *dhole* is rich red, with a darkish muzzle and a darker back-half to its bushy tail. A big male weighs up to 45 lbs and stands over 20 inches at the shoulder.

In Chitwan the wild dogs inhabit forests and perhaps cover a large area, but their numbers in the park are very low, and they are usually seen in pairs. They hunt in small packs by day, and animals as large as sambar are fair game: these efficient killers have been known to drive a deer into water before tearing it apart. A pack of wild dogs is more than a match for a tiger or a leopard. E. P. Gee records how a tiger took refuge in a tree when harassed by wild dogs. Unlike true canids, which have ten teats, wild dogs have twelve to fourteen, and do not bark like domestic dogs. Their gestation period is about sixty to seventy days, and from four to six

blind and helpless young are born in a litter. Once weaned, the cubs are fed on regurgitated food and when strong enough they join the pack in hunts.

Asiatic Jackal *(Canis aureus) Nepali: Syal*

A close relative of the wolf (*Canis lupus*), the jackal is only half the size of a wild dog and may stand 16 inches high at the shoulder. Its present range extends from Morocco to Kenya and from the Balkans through to Thailand. Its colour varies considerably and is a mixture of black, grey, brown and tawny.

Within the park jackals inhabit all the various environments but prefer the grasslands, where they hunt ground-roosting birds and small mammals at night. Although they are the commonest scavengers in the area, they have never been known to come to the tiger and leopard kills at the baiting sites, perhaps because of the regular presence of the big cats. Jackals also feed on fallen fruit and raid sugar-cane and corn fields in the villages.

At Tiger Tops they often come right into the camp at night, and their weird, long-drawn-out howling seems to disconcert the elephants, who begin trumpeting and growling in reply. The cacophony usually goes on for several minutes, to the alarm of some of the guests in the lodge. Experiments have shown that the elephants can be set off by a recording of jackal voices: why they dislike the noise so much, nobody is sure.

The Chitwan jackals are generally seen in pairs or family groups. They breed throughout the year, producing from four to six young in a litter after a gestation period of about two months. In March 1982 one pair gave birth to four cubs in a drain at Tiger Tops, but had to abandon their prefabricated den a month later when an unusually heavy rainstorm flushed them out. Three of the cubs disappeared; the fourth was captured and kept at the lodge for a while, but then released.

Indian Fox *(Vulpes bengalensis)*

The smallest canid of Chitwan, the Indian fox is found throughout the subcontinent: a lithe grey animal that weighs 5 or 6 lbs and lives in burrows with many openings. Nocturnal in habit, it hunts small animals and also feeds on insects and fruit. Its gestation period is about fifty days, and from two to six cubs are born in a litter. It is a creature of the open plains, and may be seen near the airfield at Meghauli.

BEARS

Sloth Bear *(Melursus ursinus) Nepali: bhalu*

Among the three species of bear found in Nepal, only the sloth bear occurs in Chitwan. The brown bear (*Ursus arctos*) and the Himalayan black bear (*Selenarctos thibetanus*) both live at higher altitudes, although reports persist that the latter was found in Chitwan until recent times.

Sloth Bear cubs

The first skin of a sloth bear was wrongly identified in 1791 as that of a sloth — a sluggish, tropical American mammal. But in 1793 the species was classed as a true bear, and it has since been known as the sloth bear. Adult males standing on their hind legs can be 5'8" to 6 feet tall and weigh up to 300 lbs; females are much smaller. They have shaggy black coats with a white 'V' or a crescent on the chest, and pale-yellow, elongated muzzles.

Essentially forest animals, they are found throughout the subcontinent, including Sri Lanka. They feed on insects, flowers, honey, fruit and even carrion, but their staple diet consists of termites. These they get by opening up termite-mounds with their powerful claws and sucking out whole colonies with their long muzzles, which evolution has adapted for that purpose. They also climb trees readily in search of food and occasionally scavenge on tiger kills.

At close quarters they are unpredictable and they are rated among the most dangerous animals in the park, since they are liable to attack if they feel cornered. Their gestation period is six or seven months, and they do not hibernate in winter. In Chitwan mothers with one or two cubs are commonly seen during spring. Females carry their young cross-wise on their backs; older cubs stay close to the mother, climbing on to her back at the first sign of danger.

HYENAS

Scientifically speaking, hyenas are placed half-way between the felids (cats) and canids (dogs). Anatomically they are much closer to the cats, but they share the long-distance running abilities of the dogs. There are three species in the world: the striped hyena, described below, the spotted hyena (*Crocuta crocuta*) and the brown hyena (*Hyaena brunneus*). The last two are found only in Africa, where they have been well studied, but little comparable research has been done on the Indian hyena.

Striped Hyena *(Hyaena hyaena)*

Although widely distributed from India to northern Africa, this animal is rare in Chitwan, and is perhaps only an occasional visitor from the east. The truth is that the terrain of the park does not particularly suit it: the hyena is essentially a creature of the open plains, where its tireless running ability can be deployed. It does not need the dense cover of the jungle, and is not at home in a closed environment. The huge expanses of the Terai, immediately south of Chitwan, suit it much better.

A big male striped hyena stands some 3 feet at the shoulder and weighs about 90 lbs. Its large head and strong forequarters, emphasised by a dorsal mane of long hair, tail away towards deceptively weak-looking hindquarters. Its coat is dirty, dull yellow-grey with black cross-stripes.

Hyenas are best known as *the* traditional scavengers, but they are also competitive predators. Besides feeding on carrion, they hunt small and medium-sized ungulates and other animals. Essentially nocturnal, they operate singly, in pairs, or in small groups of three to six. Their powerful jaws are adapted for crushing large bones and the coarser remains of a carcass usually left behind by other carnivores. Their digestive juices are so potent that they

can dissolve solid bone and absorb the organic protein from it — an ability which most carnivores lack.

The tracks of their forefeet are much larger than those of their hindfeet — a distinctive feature which can be very useful as a means of indirect identification.

Local ignorance about wildlife was strikingly demonstrated not long ago when a report reached me that a tiger had been washed up dead out of one of the rivers. When I went to see the corpse I found it was that of a hyena — and when I remarked to the villagers that this was a most unusual kind of tiger, they defended themselves by saying, 'Well — it has a yellow body and black stripes . . .' and thought they were near enough right.

6 Elephants

Asiatic Elephant *(Elephas maximus) Nepali: Hatti*

Fifty years ago wild elephants were common in Chitwan. E. A. Smythies records how the Vice-Regal tiger hunt of 1938 was much hampered by the attentions of a big tusker, who was eventually captured amid great celebrations. Now, alas, the chances of seeing a wild elephant in the valley are extremely slim. A small herd was recently reported near Amuwa, inside the park, but the total population in Nepal is thought to be only between thirty and fifty, scattered in tiny groups along the country's southern border.

Even so, elephants play an integral part in the life of any tourist visiting Tiger Tops, for the lodge maintains a corps of twelve domesticated, trained animals, which are in action every day of the tourist season, ferrying people to and from the airfield or moving gently through the grassland and jungle on game-spotting safaris. They live in a compound of their own a couple of minutes' walk from the lodge, and a visit to their lines is a highlight of every tourist's stay.

For me — as I think for many people — the most fascinating thing about an elephant is its readiness to co-operate with man. That the biggest animal on earth should be willing to work with puny humans is somehow tremendously attractive. If it so wished, an elephant could kill its keeper with one blow of its trunk, and if it did not want to work, no human being could make it. Yet the fact is that most elephants not only co-operate, but seem positively to enjoy their association with man. They recognise their keepers easily, and if they ever need surgical treatment, they seem to realise that it is for their own good. Conversely, their keepers become extremely fond of them: some men sing to their elephants as they go along, and others believe that the great beasts understand not merely the twenty or thirty routine words of command, but everything said to them.

Over 350 fossil forms of Proboscideans are known to have existed in the world — mammoths, mastodons and elephants — but the only two that survive are *Loxodonta africana* of Africa and *Elephas maximus* of India. In spite of its Latin name, the Indian elephant is not the biggest: the African bush elephant is larger, the maximum known weight being over 6 tons, compared with the Asian elephant's 5 tons. The many differences between the two are easiest set out in tabular form:

	Asiatic	*African*
Back:	Convex	Concave
Forehead:	Double-domed	Slopes straight forward
Ears:	Roughly the shape of a map of southern India. Top edge folds forward with age.	Bigger, roughly the shape of Africa. Top edge folds backward.
Trunk:	Relatively smooth, ending in one finger on the front.	Transversely furrowed, giving segmented appearance; ends in two fingers.
Tusks:	Females have none. Some males have none.	Both sexes have them, with few exceptions.
Toenails:	Five on forefoot, four on hind.	Four and three.

Adult Asiatic males average 9 feet at the shoulder, and females 8 feet. Tuskless males — called *Makhnas* in India — generally have extra-big necks, heads and trunks, and are reputed to be exceptionally powerful. The large, leathery ears (which are profusely supplied with blood vessels on the posterior surface, and are used for thermo-regulation) fold forward along the top as the animal grows older. In advanced age the fold becomes pronounced, and the ear simultaneously loses pigmentation along the edges, turning pinkish-white. Depigmentation also sets in along the trunk, especially at the tip, on the face and behind the ears, so that the whole head seems gradually to turn paler, like a human going grey.

A few rare animals, however, lack normal pigmentation altogether: these are the celebrated white elephants which for centuries have been considered sacred by Hindus and Buddhists.

Elephants may lose some heat by sweating, but considering their vast bulk, dissipation of body-heat is indeed a problem, and it is no wonder that they take readily to water. If no water is available, they resort to the habit of inserting their trunk-tips into their mouths and spraying themselves with a saliva-like liquid — which can be of some inconvenience to anyone perched on their backs. After a bath in water they usually indulge in a dust or mud-bath, which not only cools them (the lighter colour of mud absorbing less heat than their dark skin) but also keeps insects away, since the mud dries to form a protective coating on parts of the body. Depending on the colour of the mud or clay that they have wallowed in, they appear quite a different hue from their normal dark grey, especially when seen from a distance.

To support their massive body weight, they have thick, pillar-like legs. At a normal walking pace the sequence of limb-movements enables the elephant to take its weight on three legs through most of its stride. At a fast pace, however, such as when charging or in flight, the weight is borne alternately by the legs on one side and then by those on the other; but the animal cannot run like this for more than a few minutes. An elephant's normal speed of travel is approximately 2½ miles per hour. Over short distances it is capable of impressive bursts of speed, but, technically, it cannot trot, canter or gallop and its sprightliest gait can be likened to a fast, rolling shuffle. It is said that a deep trench 7 feet wide with vertical walls is impassable to any elephant.

They rest and sleep standing on all four legs, although they relax their legs by lifting them off the ground one at a time. They may also lean against a support. Occasionally they lie down on their sides, but only for short periods (usually no more than an hour), since their weight can damage their delicate internal organs in the prone position. They are said to sleep one to three hours a day only.

An interesting method of calculating the height of an elephant is approximately twice the circumference of the forefoot. This is not 100 per cent accurate, but it is nevertheless very useful in estimating the heights of elephants from their tracks. But because of their mode of walking — the hindfoot landing in the print of the forefoot, unless they are going fast — it is not easy to obtain clear forefoot tracks.

One has to see them negotiate steep banks and hillsides to appreciate how surefooted they are; occasionally they slip and fall, especially when panic-stricken, but this happens very rarely. They are good swimmers, but suspicious of fast currents when the rivers swell and of the quicksands that develop along water-courses during the monsoons. They usually refuse to expose themselves unnecessarily to perils such as these, and show some intelligence in avoiding bridges that are not likely to support them. But their intelligence has been highly exaggerated, and even the suggestion that the Asiatic elephant is more intelligent and therefore quicker to learn than the African seems questionable. Elephants do have good memories, but these, too, are often exaggerated. Nor is there any foundation for the myth of 'elephant graveyards', to which aged animals supposedly retire before they die. Whenever a large collection of bones and ivory is found, the explanation must be that some epidemic has struck down many elephants at once: the diseases from which they are known to suffer include anthrax, foot-and-mouth, elephant pox, paralysis of the trunk, mumps and pneumonia.

The weight-bearing structure which they have evolved imposes severe restrictions on bodily movement, but these have been amply compensated for by the development of the trunk. This is an extremely powerful organ and is said to be composed of over 40,000 muscles. An elephant's sense of smell is excellent, and the nostrils at the tip of the trunk constantly pick up olfactory signals from the environment. The trunk is a multipurpose instrument, used in procuring food, drinking water and spraying its owner, in vocalisations, displays and attack, and as a main tactile organ which has increased significance during the mating period.

At birth an elephant can do nothing with its trunk, which is clumsy and unco-ordinated, but as the animal grows older it puts the limb to good use. Until it was about nine months old a baby elephant born at Tiger Tops drank water directly with its mouth, either kneeling down or standing in the river. Eventually it learnt to drink by sucking water up its trunk, raising its head, and then squirting or draining the liquid down its throat.

Elephants also use their trunks for wielding tools. For instance, they sometimes pick up a stick to scratch themselves, or use a branch to drive away insects, and they even throw mud, stones or branches at intruders. They also shake out the earth from roots of grass by hitting each bunch against their raised forefoot before putting the grass in their mouth.

The amount of food and water needed by adults is prodigious: at least 500 lbs of green fodder a day, and perhaps 45 gallons of water. The reason they eat so much is that their diet is low-protein and fibrous, consisting mainly of tall grass, and they have a low digestive efficiency, estimated at only 40 per cent. To get their daily requirement of food in the wild, they may forage for fifteen hours or more.

Ideally, they live in open, deciduous forests with an abundance of lush tall grass, but they also inhabit evergreen forests, and are much given to wandering in search of food, especially when the supply of forage varies from one season to another. Such seasonal migrations — which require vast stretches of forest — are becoming ever more difficult. As the forests disappear, and the elephants are trapped in relatively small areas, they are more and more likely to enter cultivated fields and destroy crops, so that conflict with man becomes inevitable.

They regularly visit mineral-licks to obtain the vital elements and salts that their bodies require. In the dry season, when surface water is not available in many parts of their range, they intelligently select moist spots on dried-up riverbeds and dig holes up to 3 feet deep with their feet and trunk, to obtain underground water. In this way they make water available also to a host of other animals that share their habitat.

An elephant goes through six sets of molars in its lifetime, each set having four teeth, one on each half-jaw. The molars travel forwards until they are fully worn, and are then cast out. Meanwhile new ones grow alongside them from the alveolar pockets. Every succeeding molar is larger than its predecessor and also has a longer life-span. The last one, which appears at the age of thirty to thirty-five, is fully worn out at around sixty to seventy years. By that stage the elephant can no longer chew its food properly and eventually dies of starvation — although in fact most die of various other causes (disease or injury) well before that age. There is no foundation for the belief that elephants live for hundreds of years.

The upper incisors are modified into tusks, which in all females and many males of the Asiatic species remain very small and are known as tushes. Tusks are effective weapons of offence and defence, and in the wild are usually kept sharp through constant rubbing. It is for its tusks, which provide the ivory of commerce, that the African elephant has been wantonly slaughtered throughout its range.

Nearly all African ivory is eventually imported or smuggled into Asia for carving. India has traditionally obtained ivory from Africa for hundreds of years, but the Indian trade has been badly hit recently by the prohibitive increase in the price of imported ivory. African ivory is said to be soft compared with Asian, but also less likely to crack.

In Asia, because of religious sentiments (which prevent Hindus killing animals) and also because only some males have tusks, elephants have suffered less at the hands of poachers. Reports persist, however, that in South India the proportion of tuskers in the wild population is rapidly going down as a result of selective poaching.

Not all of the tusk is visible; the base is embedded in the skull, often up to 3 feet deep. The skull itself is very large but not of solid bone: large sinuses inside make it lighter, while still providing adequate surface area for the attachment of the strong muscles that connect the head with the body via the thick, shortened neck. The hollow skull accounts for the loud sound produced when an elephant is hit on the head with the iron *ankush* by its keeper to correct it or make it pay attention.

Wild elephants live in herds, most herds being families, composed of females and their offspring. When male subadults attain sexual maturity around ten to fifteen years of age they are pushed out to the fringes of the herd and eventually separate to live on their own or in association with other bulls (all-bull herds of up to five animals are not uncommon). Despite their sexual capability, it is unlikely that they are regarded as sociologically mature until much later. The competition for receptive females is so strong that males below twenty-five years probably contribute little, genetically. Males associate with herds briefly to attend to the females on heat. A dominant bull may assume temporary leadership of the herd, but the real leader is always an elderly cow, the matriarch. In times of scarcity of food the herd may break up into smaller units and rejoin later. Where resources are plentiful, aggregations of over one hundred animals are common.

In Sri Lanka McKay recorded that a herd is sometimes divided into a nursing unit composed of females with infants — who obviously cannot keep up with the rest — and a juvenile care unit, each of which may be further divided into subunits, depending on their size. A nursing female may also nurse an infant other than her own.

Males detect females on heat by the scent originating from the latters' genitals. Females are polyoestrous — that is, they may come on heat several times in a year, and during oestrus, when they are sexually receptive, several matings may occur. Gestation lasts about twenty-two months, and usually one hairy calf is born at a time, weighing about 200 lbs and standing 3 feet at the shoulder. A female's two breasts are tucked into the space between her forelegs, and the baby drinks with the side of its mouth, rather than with its trunk. Babies depend on their mothers' milk for up to four years, by which time they will have taken to a full vegetarian diet, but the association between mother and calf is prolonged for years, and several calves of different ages may be seen with the mother at the same time.

A phenomenon closely related with the sexual activity of the male Asiatic elephant is musth. During musth the temporal glands between the eye and the ear swell up, and an oily liquid oozes out of the opening. Even trained animals become highly aggressive and intractable, refuse to obey commands, and have been known to kill people, including their own keepers. During the latter part of musth urine-dribbling occurs, and it seems that both this and the temporal gland discharge may be used as scent signals. Healthy males come into musth annually, and although a majority of them show sexual interest, others may be quite indifferent towards females. Musth lasts from two weeks to several months.

Jainudeen, McKay and Eisenberg, who investigated musth in Sri Lanka for the Smithsonian Institute, suggested that it may be a 'physiological correlate of rut', induced by sexual activity. They also suggest that musth may give the male temporary dominance over others, thereby enhancing his 'reproductive success'. African elephants of both sexes secrete from the temporal glands, but of the Asiatic species only bulls do so, with just a very occasional cow also experiencing musth.

MEN AND ELEPHANTS

In the Indian subcontinent the tradition of working with elephants is many centuries old. Elephants have been recruited into Indian armies for thousands of years, and until recently they were extensively used for logging operations in many parts of Asia, notably Burma. A few are employed for forestry to this day. The continuous demand for domestic elephants has kept alive the traditional skills of capturing and training — although now, with the decline in demand, old practices are liable to die out.

The most widely-known method of capture is the *khedda* (*kraal* in Sri Lanka), said to have been developed by the Portuguese. In this manoeuvre wild elephants are driven into a stockade by trained elephants and their riders; the animals selected for retention are restrained by chaining them to trees, and the others are released. The captives are wild and aggressive at first, but they soon calm down, and in only two or three weeks they are quiet enough for a trainer to ride on their neck. So accommodating is an elephant's temperament that even an adult, which has lived wild all its life, can become fully trained and reliable after six months or so. (The idea that only Asiatic elephants can be trained is a popular misconception: *any* elephant can be trained, but the fact is that no similar tradition of working with man has ever developed in Africa. The Ptolemies of Egypt and the Carthaginians used African elephants in the armies of antiquity, but the skill of training them died out in the Middle Ages. In the early 1900s Belgians began to train African forest elephants in the Congo, but gave up a few decades ago).

With the exception of the baby, all the trained elephants at Tiger Tops were bought in India. Prices range from the equivalent of 1,000 to 10,000 US dollars. Once a status symbol of the kind that every well-off Indian would like to possess, a domesticated elephant has now become such an expensive liability that many former owners have settled instead for cars or Jeeps. (At Tiger Tops it costs at least 2,000 US dollars to maintain one elephant for a year.) Not that high maintenance costs are anything new: it is said that in the good old days if a Maharajah wanted to ruin his ministers, he would present them with elephants. Protocol obliged the recipients to take every care of their royal gifts, but in the process there was a good chance of their going bankrupt.

Each of the Tiger Tops elephants has three keepers: in descending order of seniority, the *phanit*, the *pachhuwa* and the *mahut* (in India the order is reversed, the *mahut* being the most senior). In Nepal it is the *phanit* who normally rides the elephant, sitting on its neck, with his bare feet hooked under the neck-band, so that he can give it signals behind the ears with his toes. It is he who knows the elephant best and has most control over it. The *pachhuwa* and the *mahut* help look after it, bringing it fodder in the camp, taking it out to graze in the long grass, giving it river baths in the summer, and so on. All three men live and sleep alongside the elephant lines, and so are constantly in touch with their charge.

Domesticated elephants understand between twenty and thirty words of command, from *baith* (sit down), *sut* (lie down) to *mail* (stand up) and *utha* (pick up). This last is sometimes used when the elephant is on the move and the *phanit* or one of the passengers drops something — but several of the elephants are now so professional that they will pick up a fallen glove or pair of sunglasses with their trunk and return it to the driver without any command at all.

The camp elephants work hard for their living, often carrying up to five people for four hours a day, and by the end of a tourist season they are glad of the rest that the monsoon brings. While working each is fed a daily supplement of 25 lbs of paddy (unhusked rice), cooked or raw and seasoned with salt and molasses. Handfuls of the mixture are carefully wrapped in grass and made into a hundred or so bundles. To see an elephant accepting these treats one at a time from its keeper, and crunching them gratefully in its mouth, is a charming sight.

One problem of the elephant compound at Tiger Tops is the immense amount of dung deposited daily. A few years back someone conceived the bright idea that it should be possible to produce methane from it, so a plant was built in the hope of generating energy on the spot. Unfortunately the scheme was still-born, for it turned out that the elephants digested their food so little that the dung produced hardly any gas.

Another problem — though only an intermittent one — is that of musth. In November 1981 a large tusker called Prem Prasad came into musth at Kasara, the park headquarters. He severely injured a female elephant and remained intractable for about two weeks, although his aggressive phase lasted well over a month. He could be brought under control only after being severely jabbed with spears and kept without food for several days. He had been pensioned off for many years as he was considered too old, at about fifty-five or sixty, for active work. As soon as the onset of musth is detected, the animal is restrained with chains and put on a reduced diet, in the belief that this will lower its physical condition and accelerate its return to normal. Fortunately, no male at Tiger Tops has yet come into musth.

Domesticated working elephants do not seem to breed very well. At Tiger Tops sporadic matings have been observed over the years since 1965, but only one calf has been born — and that took everybody by surprise. Until the baby actually arrived, one night in February 1980, nobody had known for sure that its mother, Durga Kali, was pregnant. Her breasts had been swollen for the past three months, but there had been no other indication that a birth was imminent.

The birth took place soon after midnight. Unfortunately no human saw it, but the whole elephant camp became aware of the new arrival, and tremendous trulmpetings started. Rup Kali, a close associate of Durga Kali, broke loose from her chains and was evidently most anxious to be near the mother; she was chained back to her own post after great difficulty.

In a wild herd, where all the females are related to one another, some have been known to assist the mother in childbirth. It seems most unlikely that Durga Kali and Rup Kali can be related, so their behaviour was as puzzling as it was interesting. No one could tell if Rup Kali was reacting instinctively, or whether it was sheer curiosity that made her so frantic to be at the mother's side. To this day she stays close to the mother and calf whenever possible, and behaves like an aunt in the wild.

Now the calf is causing problems in his own right. For three years he has kept his mother from working. Soon he will have to be weaned and sent to be educated at the Government elephant camp at Sauraha, in the east. No matter how quickly he learns, he will not be fit to carry tourists until he is about fifteen. Only then will he have the physical strength and the nerve to stand his ground in the face of an angry tigress or a charging rhino — and by then he will have cost a great deal of money. With luck his working life will last at least forty years, from fifteen to fifty-five, and he should live on in retirement for another ten years after that.

The question of what to do with aged elephants also poses difficulties. On moral and emotional grounds the park staff would find it very hard to shoot one. Yet, equally, they cannot turn an old stager loose, for an elephant so familiar with human beings might prove a danger to villagers.

Thousands of years ago, before the Sahara became a desert, the African elephant ranged through the whole of the continent. Now it is found only south of the Sahara, its numbers drastically reduced by poaching and by the destruction of its habitat. In Asia the story is exactly the same. The most recent overall survey, by Dr R. Olivier, published in 1978, estimated that between 28,000 and 42,000 Asiatic elephants survive, with a distribution as follows:

1. *Indian subcontinent (India, Nepal, Bhutan, Bangladesh)*: 9,950-15,050
    a. West sub Himalayan foothills: 550
    b. Peninsular India (Western Ghats): 4,500
    c. Central Peninsular India: 900-2,000
    d. North-eastern India: 4,000-8,000

2. *Continental South-east Asia: 11,100-14,600*
    a. Burma: 5,000
    b. China: 100
    c. Thailand: 2,500-4,500
    d. Kampuchea, Laos, Vietnam: 3,500-5,000

3. *Island and Peninsular South-east Asia: 7,330-12,330*
    a. Andaman Islands: 30
    b. Borneo: 2,000
    c. Malaya: 3,000-6,000
    d. Sri Lanka: 2,000-4,000
    e. Sumatra: 3,000

After a visit to Chitwan in 1980 His Majesty the King of Nepal directed that a feasibility study should be put in hand for extending the national park to the east, possibly as far as Amlekhganj, so as to set aside a greater area for wildlife and to resettle the Padampur *panchayat,* which had been stricken by acute economic losses from wild-animal damage to crops. The eastern extension would include the Thori-Shikaribas area, where a remnant population of about a dozen elephants has been reported, and funds are being sought from the World Wildlife Fund for a survey of this region.

If the extension goes ahead, it will give wild elephants a new chance in Chitwan. But these mighty animals will need all the space that humans can possibly afford them, as well as sympathetic human management, if they are to survive into another century.

7 Civets and mongooses

(VIVERRIDS)

Spotted Linsang *(Prionodon pardicolor)*

Found from Nepal eastwards to Indochina, these long-bodied, short-limbed animals are also known as tiger civets. Their coat is tawny yellow, with large black spots. Of their total length of about 30 inches, nearly half is the tail, which has nine black and white rings. Linsangs hunt small mammals and birds both on the land and on trees. They are said to breed twice a year producing two young each

time. This animal is only rarely seen in the park, and unlike other civets it has no scent glands.

Large Indian Civet *(Viverra zibetha)*

The large Indian civet can be distinguished from its smaller counterpart by the erectile crest of black hair that runs along the middle of its back. It is distributed from India and South-east China

to Malaysia. The coat is grey mixed with light brown, and full-grown animals may be 4 feet long. The tail is ringed broad black and narrow white, and there are prominent black-and-white markings on the neck.

Civets are partial to scrub forest and are said to breed twice a year, with from two to four young each time. They are nocturnal and solitary hunters of small mammals, birds and reptiles, but they also eat roots and fruit. It is their highly-developed perineal glands that secrete the civet used commercially in medicines and perfumes.

Small Indian Civet *(Viverricula indica)*

This is the species most widely used for the extraction of civet: a few special commercial farms have been established. In the wild the animal is found from India and South China through to Bali. It is usually less than 3 feet long overall, and a third of this is the tail, which has from six to nine black and white rings. Its greyish coat has longitudinal rows of spots that merge into continuous lines along the back.

The civet prefers villages to forests, and feeds on small animals, vegetables and fruit at night. Females give birth to litters of from three to five young in a burrow.

Common Palm Civet *(Paradoxurus hermaphroditus)*

An animal of South and South-east Asia, the 'toddy cat' derives its name from its habit of drinking toddy juice collected in pots from palm trees in India. A greyish civet with faint, broken, longitudinal markings on the back, a black end to its tail, and a dark muzzle with a white patch below each eye, it averages 4 feet long, including the tail.

These nocturnal creatures have adapted to live near settlements, where they hunt rodents and raid poultry and planted crops. They are said to breed in holes in trees, bearing from two to four young in a litter. Besides the strong-smelling secretion of their perineal glands, their anal glands produce obnoxious fluids for use in defence.

MONGOOSES

Common Mongoose *(Herpestes edwardsi)*
Nepali: nyauri

Famous as it is for tackling snakes, the common mongoose does in fact usually come off best in fights with dangerous snakes for two reasons — first, its incredible agility, and second, its ruse of erecting its hair, which makes it look considerably larger than it is and so

often causes the snake to miss its strike on the flesh. Also, like wild pigs, mongooses are said to have some natural resistance to snake venom.

The common mongoose is found from Iraq to India. It is a mixed grey colour and has a total body-length of up to 3 feet, half of which is tail. An animal of open scrub forests, it hunts rodents, birds and so on, and also feeds on vegetable matter. In Chitwan it is occasionally seen scavenging at the remains of tiger kills. It is a prolific breeder, and may produce up to three litters in a year, each pregnancy lasting two months.

Crab-eating Mongoose *(Herpestes urva)*

This mongoose leads an amphibious existence, hunting fish, crabs and frogs in water, and it is known to break shells by hitting them

against rocks to get at the flesh inside. It measures some 2'6'' from nose to tip of tail, weighs up to 7 lbs and has a distinctive appearance: a greyish-black body with white stripes running along the sides of its face, neck and shoulders, and a naked tip to its tail.

When attacked, it defends itself by squirting a jet of stinking fluid from its well-developed anal glands.

Small Indian Mongoose *(Herpestes auropunctatus)*

This is a rare animal in the park, but its distribution ranges from Iraq through northern India to Malaysia. Mixed brownish in colour, it is about 20 inches long and lives on rodents, reptiles and insects, which it hunts by day.

8 Strange mammals

PANGOLINS

Chinese Pangolin (*Manis pentadactyla*)
Nepali: Sal macca

The scaly anteater is an extraordinary product of evolution, found from Nepal and Thailand to South-east China and Taiwan. It is perfectly adapted for preying upon ants and termites, and because of its exclusive diet of insects it does not have any teeth.

Its tongue, originating from the stomach and controlled by muscles attached to the pelvis, can be protruded up to 10 inches into nests of ants and termites; insects captured on its sticky surface are selectively swallowed, the debris apparently being separated out by the throat, whose rhythmic movements act as a filter.

A large anteater is over 3 feet long. Its body is armoured on the

back and sides by grey-brown, overlapping scales (a modified form of hair). The outsides of the limbs are similarly protected, but other areas of the body are covered with coarse hair.

The anteater is a good climber, and uses its prehensile tail in its arboreal activities. It finds food by scent and digs the site with the powerful claws on its forefeet. When threatened or attacked it curls into an impregnable ball, which even tigers do not bother with. Usually one young is born at a time, and the baby is carried by the mother on her back and tail.

The animal is said to have once been quite common in Chitwan, but it is very rare nowadays. The surviving pangolins seem to live along forest streams; they are night feeders, and by day they sleep in burrows up to 15 feet deep. Their scales are said by the Chinese and other peoples of Asia to have medicinal properties.

CHIROPTERA

Bats are true flying mammals, a literal translation of their generic name being 'hand-wing'. They are classified according to their diet into the fruit-eating *Megachiroptera* and the insect-eating *Microchiroptera*. It is this second, smaller genus which has the famous sonar system for guidance in darkness as well as three extra hearing aids: the tragus and antitragus (small cartilaginous structures on the outer ear, which make it more sensitive), and the nose-leaf — a skin-fold which also magnifies sound-waves. As their special equipment would suggest, these insectivorous bats are generally nocturnal, and essentially animals of the forest. The fruit bats, in contrast, come out in the open to feed early in the evenings and have good eyesight. Many small bats roost in hollow trees or beneath the bark.

Only a few species of bats have so far been recorded in Chitwan, but there are doubtless many more, and the whole group needs to be studied. Nepalis on the whole do not like bats (which they call *chamera*) any more than they like owls, and to go looking for such nocturnal creatures would strike most people as both eccentric and inauspicious.

Great Eastern Horseshoe Bat *(Rhinolophus luctus)*

So highly developed is the nose-leaf in this bat that it overlaps the creature's mouth, giving it a grotesque appearance. The protuberance is the shape of a horseshoe — hence the name. The long body fur is grey-black or brown. One of this insectivorous species was trapped in a butterfly net inside the tiger blind at Dhakre. Its forearm measured 2.8 inches. Horseshoe Bats roost singly   in pairs and can be seen hunting insects in the evening, flying low in the forest. Their distribution extends from India through Thailand and Malaysia to Sulmatra, Java and Kalimantan.

The following nose-leaf bats may also occur in Chitwan and the adjoining areas, but at this stage their presence is purely conjectural: intermediate horseshoe bat (*R. affinis*); Pearson's horseshoe bat (*R. pearsoni*); least horseshoe bat (*R. pusillus*); Blyth's horseshoe bat (*R. lepidus*); and large-eared horseshoe bat (*R. macrotis*).

Except for the first two, which have forearms up to 2 inches long, these are all very small, with forearm lengths usually less than 1.7 inches.

Indian Pipistrelle *(Pipistrellus coromandra)*

Another insectivorous species, sometimes encountered inside the tiger blinds, these are dark brown and very small, with forearm measuring about 1¼ inches or less.

Also likely to occur in Chitwan is an even smaller bat, the Pigmy pipistrelle (*P. minus*), which is mixed grey in colour. These hunt early in the evenings, preferring forested areas, and have an erratic flight. They are said to hibernate in winter.

Painted Bat *(Kerivoula picta)*

With their bright orange bodies and orange-and-black wings, the painted bats are unmistakeable. By day they roost in trees and conceal themselves well among dead leaves, so perhaps it is not surprising that only a few sightings have been reported in the park.

They are slightly larger than the pipistrelles, and have a forearm length of 1.4 inches or more.

Fulvous Fruit Bat *(Rousettus leschenaulti)*

These medium-sized, brownish fruit-eating bats are seen during the monsoons. Their forearms are 3 inches or more, and their range extends from Pakistan to Indochina (except Malaysia) and they are also found in Java. They have large eyes, and are said to locate food by scent.

Ratel *(Mellivora capensis)*

The ratel or honey-badger is one of the most elusive animals in Chitwan — so much so that none of the park staff nor any visitor has ever set eyes on one. Until a pair took a picture of themselves by

treading on the pressure-plate of a camera set up in the jungle by Dr McDougal to photograph tigers, their presence was unsuspected.

Even so, the ratel has a formidable reputation, based mainly on the fact that it seems entirely fearless. In Africa it has been known to attack lions in self-defence, and certainly in India it has on occasions seen off elephants, which are distinctly nervous of it.

A tough body and even tougher hide no doubt help give it self-confidence, but its most potent weapon is the exceptionally foul-smelling liquid secreted by glands in its skin. Tigers evidently think it best to steer clear of a creature with such an obnoxious stink: they seem to know that if they were contaminated by it, they would not be rid of it for days. Elephants, too, would rather have nothing to do with it: like many other animals, they naturally avoid it.

A big ratel is about 2'6'' long and weighs over 20 lbs. Most of its body is black, but a strongly-contrasting white band runs all down its back, from its forehead to the base of its tail. It hunts small mammals, birds and reptiles, and often digs large holes in search of food. Like a bear, it has a very good sense of smell, and claws well adapted for digging. From its habit of sometimes exhuming corpses, it is known as 'the grave-digger' — but one should point out in its defence that it does not go looking specifically for bodies: just for the meat which its keen nose has detected underground.

Gangetic Dolphin (*Platanista gangetica*)
Nepali: Susu, Sons

Of the four species of freshwater dolphins that survive in the world, two exist in Asia: the Chinese lake dolphin (*Lipotes vexillifer*) and the Gangetic dolphin. The latter is found in low numbers in the Ganges, the Brahmaputra and the Indus river systems.

It grows up to 8 feet long, cows being larger than bulls: its streamlined, spindle-shaped, dark-grey body has horizontal tail flukes, triangular pectoral fins, a rudimentary dorsal fin and some suggestion of a neck. The flattened rostrum or beak, protruding from its truncated head and lined with teeth, is perfectly adapted for feeding on bottom-dwelling crustaceans and fish.

These rare aquatic mammals have greatly-reduced eyes and a narrow slit of a blow-hole. It is the puffing sound which they make as they surface and exhale that usually betrays their presence: they come up to breathe every minute or so, and it is at these moments that they are seen. They do not seem very shy, and take little notice of boats or dug-out canoes.

Dolphins are sometimes sighted in the Narayani near its confluence with the Rapti, and at other places where the water is deep and slow. But the irrigation dam at Tribenighat has had a detrimental effect on their environment, in that it has caused the Narayani to silt up, and so has reduced the amount of deep water, which is what the dolphins like. They tend in any case to disappear in the dry months before the monsoon, and this suggests that they perform some small local migration, following the fish downstream to deeper water.

Their gestation period is eight or nine months, and usually one young is born at a time. Some native fishermen of Chitwan claim to have seen a mother dolphin lying on her back, half out of the water, nursing her baby . . . but this seems rather far-fetched. Local people are certainly much interested in dolphins, for they believe that their fat has valuable medicinal qualities when used for massage. Because they know that dolphins are mammals rather than fish, they do not hunt or kill them; but if they find one dead, they are quite prepared to use it. A story goes that once upon a time a Tharu woman was so desperate for fish that she entered into the Narayani and changed into a dolphin. Ever since, local sentiment has prevented their killing.

9 Primates and others

Common Langur *(Presbytis entellus) Nepali: bandar*

According to the Hindu epic *Ramayana*, langurs, under the monkey-god Hanuman, fought on the side of Lord Rama when he invaded Sri Lanka to rescue his wife Sita, held prisoner by Ravana. Ever since, they have been regarded as sacred and therefore are not molested by the Hindus.

The common langur is found in Nepal, India, Bhutan, Bangladesh and Sri Lanka. In Chitwan it inhabits the sal forest. It is quite a big creature, weighing 35-50 lbs; its head and body measure from 2 feet to 2'6'', and its tail is up to 3'6'' long. Most of its fur is greyish white, in contrast to its black face, hands, feet and callosities on the buttocks. Some individuals have chestnut throat, armpits and groin.

When Y. Sugiyama studied langurs' social organisation in South India during the 1960s, he found that they usually live in bisexual, or harem, troops controlled by a single adult male and occupy small home ranges. Other groups are formed entirely of males (bachelors) who periodically attack and sometimes succeed in overthrowing the dominant male(s) of the harem troops. Having taken control of a newly-occupied troop, the incoming males drive away all the subadult and juvenile males and kill all the infants. Strife for dominance follows among the new males; only one eventually remains with the females, and he automatically becomes the master of the troop. Ousted males either form their own group or join other bachelor colonies. In Chitwan harem troops are composed of ten to twenty animals and bachelor groups of five to ten, although a lone adult male was seen on the Bandarjhola Island between 1979 and 1981.

Langurs begin feeding at dawn — they are late wakers on foggy winter mornings — and after some hours of rest around midday

start again in the afternoon. Their diet consists of shoots, leaves, buds, flowers, fruits and the pith of tender branches. They retire usually before sundown and prefer to sleep through the night on the peripheral branches of tall trees. Though mainly arboreal in their habits, they sometimes — to their cost — come down to the ground: there, although always on the alert, they fall victim to leopards, their number one predators. Their alarm call at the sight of a tiger or leopard is a distinctive, hoarse cough, frequently repeated — *kha-ko-kha, kha-ko-kha.*

Every part of their anatomy is wonderfully adapted for life in the trees: their long tails for balance on branches and in mid-air; their manipulative, clasping hands, with reduced thumbs, for swift locomotion; and the elongated toes of their feet, with opposable thumbs, for firm purchase. With all these advantages, they leap from tree to tree with enviable freedom — but once I saw five of them miss their connection in quick succession and fall nearly 50 feet to the ground, luckily on to a cushion of tall elephant grass.

In Chitwan the langurs sometimes mate in winter, but very young babies are seen throughout the year; the gestation period is about six months. A small troop of six females, each with a one-to-three-week-old baby was once seen in mid-July. The baby clings to the mother's belly for the first few months and remains with her for about a year.

Rhesus Macaque *(Macaca mulatta)* Nepali: *bandar*

The rhesus monkey is much smaller than the langur: adults weigh up to 22 lbs and at the most are 3 feet long including the tail. They have yellowish-brown coats, pinkish faces and orangey-red fur on the loins and rump, which becomes pronounced in breeding animals. During the mating period the external parts of their genitals swell up and, in females, turn bright red. Their coats seem to become luxuriant after the monsoons, and their pelage is best during winter.

Rhesus monkeys are found from parts of eastern Afghanistan through northern India to Indochina and South China, but in South India their place is taken by the bonnet macaque, *Macaca radiata.* In Chitwan they live in the riverine forest and grasslands, feeding on plants and insects, more on the ground than in the trees, and congregating in large troops of fifty or more. In the park they are very shy, but around temples and railway stations in India they are exceedingly bold, having lost all fear of man. As they are good swimmers, their freedom of movement is not restricted by the presence of water, and in the sweltering days of summer they often bathe to cool off. On the Bandarjhola Island a troop of rhesus was once seen barking agitatedly from trees at a leopard which had just killed one of its members.

They can be trained to perform tricks, and some Indians make a living by holding monkey shows, thus providing cheap entertainment for the villagers. In the last few decades large-scale export of this species to the West for laboratory research has depleted its numbers in most of its former range, to the extent that some countries have recently banned or controlled the traffic.

LAGOMORPHA (HARES)

Rufoustailed Hare *(Lepus nigricollis) Nepali: Kharayo*

This hare is found only in Nepal and northern India, its counterpart in southern India and Sri Lanka being the blacknaped hare. Its total body length is about 20 inches, and it weighs up to 5 lbs. Its fur is generally light rufous brown, with light underparts. The hares inhabit the grassland of Chitwan, where tender shoots of grass are their main fare. Nocturnal feeders, they also raid village crops and vegetable farms. They are preyed upon by foxes, jackals, wild cats and mongooses. One or two babies are born at a time, and, unlike rabbits, the young at birth are furred, with open eyes, and capable of moving within a day.

RODENTS

Indian Porcupine *(Hystrix indica) Nepali: dumsi*

To the Nepalese the porcupine is a creature of special interest and abilities. Natives value both its meat and its quills for their supposed medicinal qualities; they also believe not only that it is capable of shooting its quills out backwards, like darts, as a form of attack or defence, but also that it carries water in its hollow tail-quills for its babies to drink or to sprinkle over them when they get too hot!

The porcupine's range is enormous, extending from the east of the Mediterranean to Nepal and Sri Lanka. Full-grown animals weigh over 35 lbs and may reach 3 feet in total body length. Generally brown, they are covered with long bristles on the neck and shoulders and with spines and quills on the back. The quills — a modified form of hair — are spear-shaped, ringed black (or brown) and white, and easily dislodged, whereas the large rattling quills on the tail are open-ended and all white. The quills are used as a defence against enemies. In counter-attacking, a porcupine moves backwards with great speed, piercing an adversary with its quills — the tactics which no doubt gave rise to the belief about the creature's ability to shoot the quills like missiles.

Both tigers and leopards eat porcupines, but there is disagreement among naturalists over the degree to which the carnivores relish them. Some people believe that the big cats do not much care for porcupines and taken them only when other prey is scarce; others think they kill them whenever they can. I myself hold the second view: tigers are opportunistic animals, and take whatever chance is presented them: they certainly kill porcupines in Chitwan, where other prey abounds.

In any case, to attack a porcupine is a risky business: leopards and tigers sustain severe and sometimes fatal injuries from doing so. According to the famous hunter-naturalist Jim Corbett, leopards suffer fewer casualties than tigers, since they tackle the porcupine more skilfully. One explanation may be that because the porcupine falls more into the prey class of the leopard than the tiger, the leopard has evolved better hunting strategies for tackling it. In Chitwan one male tiger was totally incapacitated by a quill in his shoulder, which became infected. When found at the guard post to the west of Tiger Tops, he was dying from starvation and weakness.

At death he weighed only 110 lbs — less than half what he should have been.

In the park porcupines inhabit the sal forest and the grasslands, but, being mainly nocturnal and resting in caves or burrows by day, they are not often seen. The best way of getting a look at one is to put some potatoes out in the grounds of a house and then visit the scene with a torch in the evening: roots, tubers, cereals, fruit and vegetables all form part of their diet. They also eat bones and the antlers of deer, which furnish them with calcium and other minerals needed for the healthy growth of their quills.

Giant Flying Squirrel *(Petaurista petaurista)*

Unlike bats, the true fliers among mammals, flying squirrels can only glide through the air — a process made possible by the elastic skin that connects their limbs. When launching themselves off, they spread their arms and legs so as to expand the membrane into a parachute, thus prolonging their leaps up to 150 feet or more as they sail swiftly from a higher to a lower point, usually from one tree to another. While approaching a destination they describe an upward curve, and the membrane, at right angles to the line of movement, efficiently checks their velocity, enabling them to land smoothly.

Giant flying squirrels have chestnut-brown bodies 16-18 inches

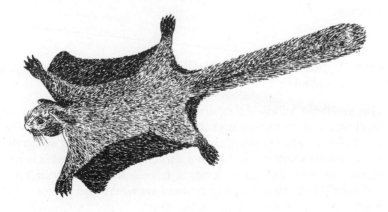

long, and thick, bushy tails up to 2 feet long. They are found in the Indian subcontinent and South China including Taiwan, through to Borneo. On light summer nights they leap from tree to tree in the sal forest in search of fruit, nuts, shoots and even the bark of some trees. They nest in holes in trees. One afternoon I saw some twenty jungle crows mobbing a squirrel, which eventually escaped by disappearing into the forest.

Particoloured Flying Squirrel *(Hylopetes alboniger)*

Blackish, with white streaks and white underparts, this small flying squirrel is found from Nepal through northern Thailand to Indochina. In Chitwan it is perhaps most numerous in the hill forests. Its head and body are about 8 inches long, and it has an equally long flattened tail.

Hoary-bellied Himalayan Squirrel
(Callosciurus pygerythrus)

Another squirrel common in Chitwan, this one is about 18 inches long including the tail. Its body is medium-brown, and its tail faintly ringed. It is usually seen at the edge of the sal forest, where it feeds on bark and fruit. Its loud, jerky call is often heard in the evenings.

Five-striped Palm Squirrel *(Funambulus pennanti)*
Nepali: lokhark

This small but handsome squirrel is brownish-grey, with five pale longitudinal stripes on its neck and back. Its head and body may be 6 inches long, and the tail slightly longer. Unlike the flying squirrels, it is diurnal and quite vocal, with a shrill bird-like call, and is rarely found away from human settlements. It feeds on flowers, fruit, bark and eggs. The gestation period is about six weeks and two or three young are born in a nest built by the female.

Indian Field Mouse *(Mus booduga)*

A dark grey-brown animal with the head and body averaging just over two inches long and a shorter tail.

House Mouse *(Mus musculus)*

The small brown rodent found all round the world, the house mouse resembles the house rat except that it is much smaller, measuring from 4 to 6 inches in length, half of which is tail. These omnivorous, nocturnal creatures are prolific breeders, producing several litters a year, with from four to six young born at a time. A one-month-old house mouse is sexually mature.

Longtailed Tree Mouse *(Vandeleuria oleracea)*

This arboreal mouse is brown with white underparts, usually about 2½ inches in body length, and has a long tail up to 4 inches or more. Its hands and feet are adapted for arboreal life, with opposable first and fifth toes ending in a nail instead of a claw. Between three and six young are born at a time in a nest built in the trees.

Common House Rat *(Rattus rattus)*

Said to have originated in South and South-east Asia, house rats have — unfortunately — achieved worldwide distribution. Their colour, varying from grey to nearly black, is basically brown. They average 14 inches long including their scaly tail, which is slightly longer than the body. Some live in the forest, but they are most numerous around human habitations, where their omnivorous appetite makes them highly destructive. They also carry disease, and are thus a major pest.

Many other species prey on them, including hawks, owls, snakes, jackals and the smaller cats, but they are so prolific that they can easily withstand this combined assault and maintain their numbers.

From time to time large-scale rat migrations take place — perhaps as a means of population control. In their paper of 1977 Lekagul and McNeely refer to two such migrations in Thailand during 1913 and 1931.

Indian Mole-rat or Bandicoot *(Bandicota bengalensis)*

These rodents — very common in the park — are a menace to cultivation in the surrounding villages, and notorious for their habit of hoarding large quantities of corn in underground stores, whence the grain is constantly retrieved by desperate farmers. As they dig their burrows, piles of fresh earth like mole-hills are thrown up at the entrance — hence their name.

The mole-rat is found in India, Nepal and Burma, and also in Java and Sumatra. Its body is about 6 inches long (excluding the tail, which is shorter) and mixed brown and grey, with paler underparts. Like the house rat it is highly prolific and breeds several times a year.

Great Bandicoot *(Bandicota indica)*

This larger relative of the mole-rat also lives in the park's grasslands and forests, but in lesser numbers. Its distribution extends from India to Taiwan and south to Java and Sumatra. Large specimens may be a foot or more in body length, excluding the thick, black tail, which is shorter, and may weigh 2½ lbs. They are generally dark-grey mixed with brown, almost black on the back but pale underneath. These and other rats are relished by the native Tharus.

Bay Bamboo Rat *(Cannomys badius)*

This chestnut-coloured rat has a cylindrical head and body up to 10 inches long, a short tail of about 2½ inches, and well-developed incisors and claws — all adaptations for underground existence. By day it shelters in burrows that lead to a spacious chamber, and it comes out to feed on roots and so on at dusk. It is found in the Himalayan foothills from Nepal eastwards through Thailand to Kampuchea.

Bay Bamboo Rat

INSECTIVORA

Grey Musk Shrew (*Suncus murinus*)
Nepali: Chhuchhundro

Because of its musky odour and rat-like appearance, this nocturnal insectivore is also known as the musk rat. It is widely distributed from the United Arab Republic and Ethiopia to South and Southeast Asia. Its head and grey-brown body measure about 6 inches, and the 3-inch tail bears a thin growth of rigid hair. These shrews are intolerant of rats, and have a proboscis-like snout, depressed ears and two distinctive front teeth. The musk glands — one on each side of the body — are said to secrete profusely during the breeding period, and females produce two litters a year, each consisting of from two to five young.

MUSTELIDS

Smooth-coated Otter *(Lutra perspicillata) Nepali: ot*

With their streamlined bodies, webbed feet, flattened muscular tails and fully-waterproof fur, the otters are perfectly-evolved aquatic predators. The smooth-coated otter has a dark-brown body, weighs up to 22 lbs, and measures 4 feet or more from nose to tip of tail.

This animal ranges from the Indian subcontinent east to Indochina and south to Sumatra, and a small population survives along the river, Tigris. Its main prey is fish, but if none is available it takes readily to hunting on land.

In Chitwan the otters are seen most often during the winter months in groups of four to eight. In summer they disappear, probably migrating northwards in pursuit of the fish, which move upstream during the monsoon floods, and also seeking a cooler environment. They appear to breed mainly in winter, and their gestation period is said to be two months. Two new-born cubs were picked up in early November 1981 and flown to the Otter Trust in England.

Indian fishermen use trained otters to drive fish into nets; they also employ them as decoys to lure freshwater dolphins, which are fascinated by the otters' squeaking and blunder into nets as they come to investigate.

Yellow-throated Marten (*Martes flavigula*)
Nepali: Malsapro

This lithe, tree-living predator is only occasionally seen in Chitwan. From nose to tail-tip it measures about 3 feet, the thick tail taking

up over a third of its length, and it varies considerably in colour, the body being generally brownish-black, with yellow fur on the throat and upper chest, but with the extent of the yellow also varying from one individual to another.

These martens, working on their own or in pairs, hunt small mammals, birds, reptiles and insects; they also eat flowers and fruit, and they have been seen from time to time scavenging on the remains of tiger kills. Their range extends from northern Pakistan to Kalimantan and north to eastern Siberia.

10 Birds

Chitwan is a paradise for bird-watchers, and one of the most rewarding places in the world for spotting and study. Although Nepal covers only a fraction of 1 per cent of the earth's land mass, it contains about a tenth of the world's known birds, and of these more than half are to be found within the national park. So far 440 species have been recorded in the park, and it is not uncommon for an experienced group of ornithologists to identify over a hundred species in the course of a single, day. Ninety-nine species were identified one morning in late February of 1979 during the 4-mile walk from Tiger Tops to the tented camp.

The reasons for Nepal's great wealth of birds are mainly topographical. First, the country has a huge variation in altitude within a short lateral distance, so that conditions range from tropical to arctic in a distance of less than 100 miles; and second, Nepal lies in the region of the overlap between the Palaearctic realm to the north and the Oriental to the south.

Except when a different source is quoted, every species listed in Appendix B has been confirmed by at least three reliable naturalists or ornithologists. About a hundred species have been added since 1977, but others have been deliberately omitted from the list until we get further confirmation of their presence. We have tentatively categorised our birds as year-round residents, winter visitors, summer visitors, passage migrants and vagrants, and we have assigned them ratings to indicate scarcity or abundance, from 1 for rare, up to 6 for very common.

Our knowledge is limited by two important factors. First, most of our bird-watching is done between mid-September and mid-June — that is, outside the monsoon period, when the lodge is closed to visitors. Second, we normally cover only a relatively small area in the west of the park — the triangle between Surung Khola (just over a mile east of Tiger Tops), the southern end of the large Bandarjhola

Island, and Golaghat, where all the channels of the Narayani unite. Sometimes our expeditions extend to Kasara and beyond in the east, and along the Narayani from Sighraulighat at the north-west tip of the park to the river's confluence with the Mohan Khola. Even so, we explore no more than a fraction of the park's huge expanse. The compensation is that the area which we do cover contains almost all the types of vegetation and habitat to be found in the park as a whole, except for the chir pine forest which grows on the higher ridges of the Churia hills.

Our bird-watching has become much more professional in recent years. Many dedicated ornithologists from all over the world, notably Great Britain, Europe and the United States, have visited Chitwan and contributed handsomely to our knowledge of the park's avifauna. These groups work with the greatest enthusiasm, going out at first light and making use of every waking hour. Even so, much work remains to be done, and there are still many discoveries to be made: because of the sheer size of the park, and its dense vegetation, one can safely bet that it contains birds never yet recorded. For the moment the statuses which we have assigned must remain provisional; so must the ratings which we have given for abundance and habitat-preference, and the list can serve only as a rough-and-ready guide.

For example, the common hawk cuckoo is seen and heard between late January and October, and has therefore been listed as a summer bird, but because of its elusive nature and silence outside the breeding period, it could easily be present and overlooked during the rest of the year. On the other hand, ospreys, which are generally believed to be wintering birds, are listed as residents since they are seen in all months and we strongly suspect that they breed in Chitwan. However, they do appear to increase in number during the winter. Again, many birds listed as residents — which therefore must breed here — are mentioned as *possible* breeders for the simple reason that we have not confirmed their nesting. Nor is it always possible to give a satisfactory abundance-status when dealing with such a large variety of birds, some of which are flocking species and some solitary. Our ratings are thus at best approximations and do not indicate the population of species so much as our chances of seeing them in the park. The grasslands, the upper sal and the hill forests all need further investigation, and many birds now listed as rare may be more common than we suppose.

Even with all these difficulties, bird-watching in Chitwan is most exciting, not least because some highly unusual vagrants have been recorded here in the past five years, among them Bewick's swan, which was new for Nepal. Other rarities include species last known to have occurred in Nepal in the middle of the nineteenth century: lesser sand plover, grey-headed fishing eagle and slender-billed babbler. This last bird was discovered in the grassland and is certainly not rare. Irregular visitors such as brown-crowned pigmy woodpecker, black-capped kingfisher and sarus crane have been sighted sporadically in some years.

The most interesting periods are September-November and February-April, when migrants arrive, depart or pass by. The numbers of wintering birds are greatly augmented by passage migrants which stop over briefly in Chitwan before moving on. Others, such as common cranes and white storks, usually overfly, the former in large numbers.

If it seems remarkable that well over half of the birds listed for Nepal should be found here, the reason is that the park's heterogeneous environment provides a multitude of ecological niches for birds to exploit. For instance, the river systems and associated bodies of water contain a wide assortment of aquatic fauna and flora, while the forest and grasslands provide flowers, nectar, fruits and seeds, as well as the ubiquitous insects.

It is fascinating to study the way in which the birds use these various food resources. Unfortunately, because of overfishing by local villagers, Chitwan supports a poor population of fishing raptors. All the same, ospreys, cormorants, darters, fishing eagles, mergansers, fish owls and white-tailed sea eagles hunt medium-to-large fish, and gulls, terns and kingfishers take smaller ones. Besides fish, the rivers, marshes and lakes support a wide array of crustaceans, molluscs, frogs, tadpoles, worms, aquatic insects, larvae, eggs and so on, which are preyed upon by herons and storks (both also take fish), bitterns, waders and crakes. Moorhens, cranes, ducks and geese feed on the same things, but are also vegetarians to a greater or lesser extent, eating roots, tubers and seeds of aquatic plants. The greylag and barheaded geese, teals, pintails, spotbills and garganey are largely plant-feeders and partial to cultivated

Brown Fish Owl *Darter*

fields, as are the common and demoiselle cranes. On the other hand, the goldeneye and the tufted duck are believed to be more dependent on animal food.

Birds of prey (including owls) hunt small mammals, birds, eggs and nestlings, besides reptiles, frogs and insects. Vultures maintain sanitation in nature by scavenging. Green pigeons are fruit-eaters, and their smaller relatives, the doves, are grain- and seed-eaters. Parakeets, which are a bit of both, do much damage to crops and orchards and are highly injurious to the local economy. Sparrows, munias, buntings and weavers feed on grass seeds, and sunbirds (which occupy an ecological niche similar to that of the New World humming birds) live on the nectar of flowers (many other birds such as spiderhunters and hair-crested drongos also use this resource).

Hornbills, barbets, orioles, mynas and bulbuls subsist mainly on fruit, but supplement their diet with insects. The reverse may be true for many of the remaining birds. Insects are hawked in the air by bee-eaters, swifts, swallows, martins and drongos; woodpeckers and nuthatches search for them on tree trunks, and wall creepers on vertical cliffs. Pittas scan through leaf litter, forktails hunt forest streams, and wagtails prey upon insects along the stream and river

Purple Sunbird

Large
Raquet-
tailed
Drongo

Giant Hornbill

Red-whiskered Bulbul

Large Golden-backed Woodpecker

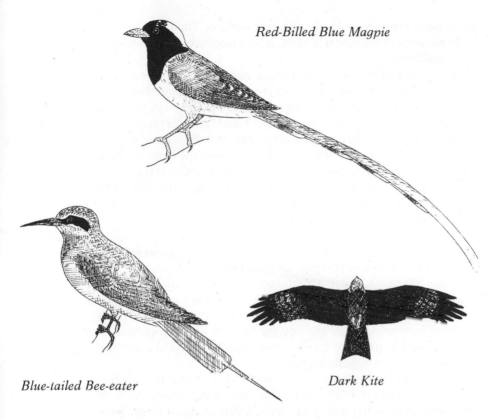

Red-Billed Blue Magpie

Blue-tailed Bee-eater

Dark Kite

beds. Bush chats, babblers, shrikes and prinias control insects in the grasslands, together with the rare rubythroat and the bluethroat, which prefer to stay on the ground. Others such as minivets and allies, flycatchers, leaf warblers and cuckoos hunt insects in the forest canopies.

Red-billed blue magpies may be seen at the tiger kills early in the mornings, and the dark kite and the house sparrow live alongside man. Elsewhere flowerpeckers are closely associated with mistletoe fruit, but this needs confirmation in Chitwan. Jungle mynas ride on rhinos, and often flocks of them betray the presence of the pachyderms in tall grass. Whether the mynas eat ticks and other parasites from the rhinos' hide is not known, but they certainly benefit by feeding on insects that fly off the vegetation as the clumsy giants crash through it. Similarly, cattle egrets and pied mynas accompany grazing herds of cows and buffalo. Thus, while some birds are highly-specialised feeders, others tend to be omnivorous in varying degrees.

At the apex of the avian food chain are the birds of prey, and apart from the vultures, which congregate in large numbers at a carcass, they are usually seen singly or in pairs. The ways in which evolution has adapted them for a life of hunting or scavenging can be seen in the make-up of their wings, tails, feet, beaks and eyes.

Their long primaries impart speed — witness the amazing pace with which a peregrine falcon stoops on its prey and overtakes it in level flight if its first dive fails. Long secondaries give breadth to the wings and are responsible for lift: the large wing-area of vultures makes them perfect gliding machines, able to ride the thermals for hours on end with very little expenditure of energy. Yet their sheer size and weight render them unwieldy in still air: a bird that is 4 feet long, with a 9-foot wing-span and weighing up to 30 lbs, has difficulty taking off, and this is why one often sees vultures perched in the tree-tops at the beginning of the day. They are waiting for the build-up of the hot-air currents that will carry them easily to high altitude, from which they can spy for food. If they are obliged to take off quickly from the ground, they launch themselves into the air after an ungainly, hopping run.

Because tails act as rudders, it is small wonder that the falcons, kestrels and harriers have long, strong tails which enable them to twist and turn swiftly after their prey. Vultures, in contrast, have very short tails, for they do not need to turn quickly. All the diurnal birds of prey have exceptionally acute eyesight.

Short tails are a feature shared by the hunters of the night, the owls. Most of these have short wings with soft flight feathers, which help them hunt silently. Their large, bulging eyes enable them to see well in the dark and are placed on the front of their heads rather than the sides. This gives them good binocular vision for judging distances accurately — a skill vital for their striking capacity. Their vision is not wide-angle, as in other birds, but this limitation is compensated for by the owls' ability to turn their heads full circle.

No less specialised are their beaks: most owls have small beaks with wide gapes, so that they can swallow prey whole. Other birds of prey have strong beaks for tearing prey apart. Most vultures have long, large beaks powerful enough to open up a carcass — but not the Egyptian vulture: its slender bill is adapted to clear up the remaining flesh from the bones, a suitable tool for a latecomer.

The raptors' killing-weapons are their powerful feet. The toes of the osprey, the fishing eagle and the fish owl have been equipped by evolution with rough undersides so that they can grip slippery fish.

In over a hundred species of birds that are seen in Chitwan, the males differ from the females in appearance — that is, they exhibit sexual dimorphism. Yet the differences, although pronounced in some, are only minor in others. As a general rule, males are more brilliantly coloured and therefore more attractive: minivets, peafowl, junglefowl, parakeets, sunbirds, woodpeckers, green pigeons, most ducks and flycatchers — all these are good examples. In the great majority of our birds, however, both sexes look alike: bulbuls, drongos, babblers and allies, leafwarblers, pipits and wagtails, bee-eaters, swifts, swallows and martins, nightjars, herons, storks, owls, vultures and, last but not least, eagles. This last group is one of the most difficult to identify accurately, and extreme caution should be exercised before a sighting is confirmed.

Courtship display — an integral part of pair-formation — varies as widely as do the species themselves. From January to May the spectacular dance of the peacock is a common sight in Chitwan: the male raises his tail-feathers vertically into a huge fan, with the iridescent moons facing forward, and pivots back and forth in a graceful pavane. Scarcely less impressive are the displays of the egrets during the monsoon. These slender, longlegged white herons raise and lower their feathers, forming white sprays round their crests and bodies, and thereby making themselves still more striking.

Another of the great sights of spring is the flight display of the crested serpent eagle. Twisting and turning and rolling in the air, each pair performs thrilling — and noisy — aerobatics. It has been suggested that such demanding aerial manoeuvres of the birds of prey are a test of physical prowess, and give the female a chance to decide whether or not she has found a competent enough male candidate, with a promising reproductive potential, before she commits herself to a relationship.

By late April most of our winter birds have gone, while others have arrived for nesting. As the breeding season begins, songsters

Grey Heron

*Crested
Serpent
Eagle*

fill the air with lovely melodies, and after dark the nightjars, owls and cuckoos sing all night long. In short, the males are competing with other males for mates, but that is not the whole story. The female painted snipe and common bustard-quail are larger and slightly brighter-coloured than the male. They are also aggressively disposed, and battle with rivals for possession of a mate. Each female then settles down temporarily with one male, but once the eggs are laid she abandons her partner in search of a new one. The docile male incubates the eggs and raises the young all by himself.

Successive polyandry is also reported among the bronze-winged and the pheasant-tailed jacanas. On the other hand, the peacock and the baya weaver are polygynous. Although some birds such as eagles and talking mynas are said to pair for life, most birds are monogamous through the season, and both sexes share domestic work.

The commonest type of nest is the regular cup-shaped or domed structure on a tree, in the grass or on the ground; but barbets, woodpeckers and parakeets nest in hollow trees, and kingfishers, bee-eaters and sandmartins in holes in riverbanks or sloping ground. Their tunnels terminate in spacious chambers and may be up to 6 feet deep. The black-bellied tern lays its eggs on bare sandbanks and the spurwinged plover among pebbles. These and other similarly-nesting birds must bring off their young before the

Black-necked Stork

Small Pied Kingfisher

monsoon floods arrive, otherwise their nests are liable to be swamped.

The openbilled stork builds a flimsy platform of twigs and nests in colonies. Egrets and pond herons nest in mixed colonies among rushes during the monsoons. The lesser adjutant stork builds a solitary nest on top of a large tree in winter.

But these are ordinary nests: some birds make much more elaborate arrangements. The rufous woodpecker excavates the nest of tree ants and uses that for breeding. The hornbill plasters his wife into the hollow of a large tree with mud and saliva, leaving a small opening through which he feeds her while she incubates the eggs. The opening is also used by the female and later by the chicks to defecate outside. At one point in the chicks' growth the female is released and the chicks walled up again until they are nearly fully grown. It is not clear how or why this extraordinary method evolved: to the human observer it seems to create a great deal of unnecessary work, and to throw a heavy strain on the male.

Another miracle of craftsmanship is the nest of the crested tree swift — a tiny saucer of pieces of wood and bark, glued together with saliva and placed inconspicuously on a branch. Baya weavers build beautifully-woven, retort-shaped structures with vertical

Crested Tree-Swift

*Red-winged
Crested Cuckoo*

tubular entrances. They breed in colonies, and some trees are fully laden with their nests, which hang freely from the branches. Although the female selects her nest for breeding, she herself does not know how to weave at all, and the work is all done by the male! The tailor bird is famous for its nest which it builds inside a container stitched out of one large leaf or from several leaves joined together. Similar nests are constructed by rufous, grey-capped and Hodgson's prinias: cobwebs and vegetable fibres are used as threads for stitching, and the ends are ingeniously knotted to prevent breaking.

Cuckoos are brood-parasitic — that is, they lay their eggs in the nests of other birds, which in this case are known as hosts or fosterers. Particular species of cuckoo are said to take advantage of particular hosts. For example, red-winged crested cuckoos often parasitise necklaced laughing thrushes, and Indian cuckoos, ashy and black drongos. But there is more to the process than just deceiving the hosts. The cuckoos' breeding season must synchronise with that of the chosen species, and their eggs usually match those of the host. Moreover, cuckoos' eggs are said to hatch more quickly than the hosts'. This perhaps enhances the parasites' chances of

*Paradise
Flycatcher*

Bengal Florican

Demoiselle Crane

survival, by depriving their smaller and weaker nestmates of their rightful share of food. Some cuckoos also habitually evict legitimate chicks from the nest. Yet not all cuckoos have such selfish nesting behaviour. The sirkeer cuckoo, the large green-billed malkhoa and the coucals of the same family all build their own nests.

Most of our wintering ducks and waders are Transhimalayan migrants, their breeding grounds extending as far north as Siberia and the Arctic circle. Some annual migrants travel vast distances. For example, a wood sandpiper ringed in India was recovered 3,900 miles away in the USSR, and ringed garganeys have flown between 3,000 and 4,000 air miles in one direction. Yet many birds are merely regional migrants, and do not travel anything like such long distances. The paradise flycatcher and the black-naped monarch flycatcher arrive for breeding in summer from within the Indian subcontinent. Wintering leafwarblers and flycatchers such as orange-gorgetted, rufous-breasted, rusty-breasted, little pied and slaty blue, are said to breed higher up in the Himalayas, and are therefore altitudinal migrants.

Still other birds use Chitwan only for a brief stopover on their way to or from their breeding grounds. These include the demoiselle crane, sooty flycatcher, curlew and spotwinged stare. This last species is said to be an east-west migrant, breeding beyond western Nepal and wintering in Assam. Another east-west migrant is said to be the redwinged crested cuckoo, which supposedly winters in Africa.

Because visibility is limited by the thick vegetation that covers the park for most of the year, it is particularly useful to memorise bird calls and songs: many species can be recognised by voice only, especially the elusive ones such as owls, nightjars and cuckoos which are active at night. Among the most popular daytime singers are the robin dayal, spotted babbler, orange-headed ground thrush, the orioles, the whistling thrush and the shama. The shama is a highly-accomplished songster, famous for the habit of changing its tune every time one tries to imitate it, and thereby making further imitations ever-more difficult.

The racket-tailed drongos are said to mimic calls and songs of many birds, from serpent eagles to koel cuckoos and jungle babblers. The talking mynas do not seem to mimic other birds in nature, but they can easily be trained, and they are considered the best imitators of the human voice, even better than parrots.

The best months for bird-watching are February and March. At this time of year a twenty-four-hour watch may produce a list of 125 species. But one should not expect to identify all the birds that one sees; a few are bound to remain mysterious. Some may be too shy to show themselves or all their features clearly for any length of time, or the light may be bad. Ordinary 8x or 10x binoculars may not pick up details of plumage, especially if the bird is at a distance. Sometimes even common birds can be problematic. For instance, many ornithologists have considerable headaches trying to differentiate between the ashy, black and crow-billed drongos.

But even the drongos must yield precedence, in terms of problem-setting, to the birds of prey. The identification of raptors, especially those that are day-flying, presents a major challenge. Because of the differences in plumage within the same species and at various stages of the moult, a positive identification is always difficult. The birds are often seen at considerable heights, and although silhouettes and wing-positions can be helpful, these too are variable and confusing. An even harder task than to identify a raptor at flight is to recognize one perched on a tree.

Yet the solution of tricky problems is what bird-watching is all about — and nowhere in the world is there an environment which presents ornithologists with a greater challenge, or greater variety, than Chitwan.

11   Reptiles and amphibians

A great variety of snakes live in the park, but because of the dense cover and their own shyness they are rarely seen. They usually keep out of man's way: as they pick up vibrations transmitted through the ground, they move off before any approaching human comes into sight. In winter, when most tourists visit Chitwan, they hibernate, and during their period of greatest activity — the monsoon — there are no visitors around to see them. The people who come across them much more are the villagers living outside the park, for snakes congregate around human habitations, drawn by the population of rats.

Most local people have a strong traditional fear of snakes, and kill them. Even otherwise reliable *shikaris* tend to regard some non-keeping down the population of rodents. They think any dark, blackish snake is a cobra, and assume that any snake-bite will kill them. Even otherwise-reliable *shikaris* tend to regard some non-venomous snakes as poisonous, and the psychological effect of snake-bite is probably greater than the chemical: more people die from the shock of being bitten than from being poisoned. They think they are bound to die, and do.

Remedies for snake-bite are of course kept at Tiger Tops. Antidotes are usually specific to a particular kind of venom, but polyvalent antidotes, good for a few species, are also available. Venom is extracted from the snake's fangs and injected into the bloodstream of a horse, in increasing doses, until the horse has become immune. Serum is then manufactured from the animal's blood, and this forms the antidote, known as antivenin.

If someone *is* bitten by a snake, it is important that the antivenin should be administered by a competent doctor. First, every attempt should be made to identify the type of snake accurately. Nepalis, tending to think that *all* snakes are poisonous, exaggerate the dangers involved; but if a person bitten by a harmless rat-snake is injected with cobra antivenin, he may well be poisoned by the attempted cure.

King Cobra *(Ophiophagus hannah)*

This largest of all the world's poisonous snakes has been known to reach a length of 18 feet, although it averages 10-12 feet. An animal of dense forests, it is rare throughout its range in the Indian subcontinent, and in the park it is seen only a few times in a year. Young king cobras have yellow-to-white bands on a black skin, but large animals gradually lose the bands and become uniformly dark olivaceous black or brown. White individuals are not unknown.

King Cobras are not nearly as aggressive as many books make them out to be, but a bite from one may result in death (often quickly) from cardiac failure and respiratory arrest. Volume for volume, the king cobra's venom is not as toxic as that of some other poisonous snakes, but it is capable of injecting quantities that might prove fatal even to an elephant. As its generic name suggests, it feeds largely on other snakes such as rat snakes. It is also the only snake known to build a proper nest of leaf-litter and twigs. The females guard their eggs by lying on top of the nest, perhaps throughout the incubation period of sixty to seventy days, until the young are born.

Common Cobra *(Naja naja)*

This snake is extremely rare in the park but quite common in the farmlands and around villages which are its favourite haunts. Usually black to light-yellowish, and from 3 to 5 feet long, it gives a spectacular warning display by expanding its neck ribs to form a wide hood, with or without markings. Its venom is neurotoxic, which means that it attacks the nervous system. Most cobra bites are not fatal to man but may cause tissue damage to the bitten part. Some common cobras can spit venom 3 feet or more, but not as far as the African spitting cobra. (Venom landing on the skin does no harm provided it is washed off quickly; but it can be dangerous if it gets into the eyes.) Defanged cobras are maintained as pets for local entertainment by Indian snake-charmers. Female cobras are said to guard their eggs until they hatch. Feeding largely on rats and other rodents, which they catch by striking with their fangs, these nocturnal predators are very wary of man.

Green Pit-Viper *(Trimeresurus albolabris)*

Among the four more poisonous snakes in the park, the green pit-viper is the one most frequently encountered. Averaging about 18 inches long, it has a triangular head which looks rather large for its body size and appears even more disproportionate because of its narrow neck. Its variable green skin serves as excellent camouflage among the thick vegetation that it prefers. The pits in front of each eye are infra-red sensors which give good night vision. These extra infra-red eyes are sensitive to heat, and probably give the snake quite a detailed picture of its prey: how big it is, what it is doing, and — most important for a successful strike — exactly how far away it is. The fangs, when not in use, fold backwards along the sides of the mouth, but while striking they are locked into place by muscular action. The green pit-viper does not lay eggs, but gives birth to four or five live young. Its reluctance to move when approached renders it quite dangerous. This nocturnal creature feeds largely on frogs, rats and mice.

Common Krait *(Bungarus caeruleus)*

Of all the poisonous snakes in Chitwan, the common krait has the most potent venom, and, as in the cobra, it is neurotoxic. Seldom exceeding 5 feet in length, the kraits average 3 feet, and are generally coloured black with a shiny, steel-blue tinge interrupted by thin white crossbands which may be broken or indistinct towards the front. They feed on other snakes, including their own kind, and also on rodents. Females are believed to stay near their eggs. Hiding in burrows and crevices by day, these night-hunters are more numerous outside the park than inside.

Indian Python *(Python molorus) Nepali: Ajingar*

This is by far the largest snake in the park. Elsewhere, pythons 20 feet long have been recorded, and in Chitwan a 14-foot specimen was seen and photographed swallowing a whole hog deer, whose body had a diameter of at least a foot and weighed some 60 lbs. But another snake, 17 feet long, was found dead, having killed itself trying to swallow an even bigger hog deer. (The snake's ability to swallow such enormous lumps of food derives from the structure of its jaws, which are connected to each other by tough, elastic muscles, and can separate widely.) A python may take five or six hours to

ingest a large prey animal completely, and after such a heavy meal it can go without food for weeks. There is one instance on record of a python in captivity living without food for over two years.

Pythons are usually found near lakes or streams, where they lie motionless, waiting for unwary prey to wander within range. Although their colours are bold — black, yellow and white — they blend to give surprisingly good camouflage. They catch animals such as hog deer by striking with their fangs and squeezing the victims to death in the coils of their powerful bodies. But mostly they feed on rodents. Infra-red-sensitive pits on their mouth-margins give them the capacity to hunt in darkness. Females lay up to a hundred eggs: one year a female was seen near Tiger Tops coiled round her eggs in late May and early June. No figures are available for the mortality of the young, but it must be exceedingly high, for pythons are long-lived (perhaps surviving for forty years) and during that time each reptile manages to produce — theoretically — an average of only one breeding successor.

Rat Snake *(Pytas mucosus)*

This harmless snake averages from 6 to 8 feet long. Its colour varies from olive-yellow to black, with black crossbars along its length, and it is sometimes mistaken for the common cobra or king cobra. It hunts rats and other rodents by day, yet its contact with man is minimal. The female lays about a dozen eggs that hatch in approximately sixty days.

Whip Snake *(Ahaetulla nasutus)*

A very large whip snake may exceed 6 feet, but half that length is more usual. It has a slim body, with an exceptionally pointed snout, and is a graceful climber. Its skin is bright parrot green, and two yellowish lines run along the sides of its belly for the length of its body — a colouration that provides perfect camouflage in the trees where it hunts lizards and small birds. It also feeds on mice and frogs on the ground. Its fangs are at the back of its jaws, and not very effective. Females give birth to six or eight young.

Wolf Snake *(Lycodon aulicus)*

Ranging from grey to very dark, the wolf snake has narrow, pale-yellow crossbands slightly resembling those of the common krait, which is much larger. Usually less than 2 feet long, wolf snakes are partial to human habitations, and feed on lizards, frogs and so on at night. They are harmless and oviparous, or egg-laying.

Cat Snake *(Boiga trigonata)*

Averaging 2'6" long, the cat snake has bulging eyes and a thin, pointed tail. The skin is brownish, with dark markings that impart a striped pattern. It is back-fanged, with a weak venom, feeds largely on lizards, mice and other small rodents, and is oviparous.

Striped Keelback *(Amphiesma stolata)*

Measuring some 18 inches (exceptionally large specimens may be twice that length), this harmless snake has a brown skin with darker bands and two yellowish lines running along the sides of its back. It preys on frogs, lizards and rodents.

Common Worm Snake *(Typhlina bramina)*

Also known as the blind snake because of its highly-reduced eyes, this earthworm-like reptile is usually chocolate to black in colour and less than 6 inches long. By day it burrows in the forest floor, coming out to hunt worms, larvae and insect eggs at night. Apparently all common worm snakes are females, reproducing parthenogenetically by self-fertilisation, and laying about half a dozen eggs. Their defence against predators is a foul-smelling chemical which their bodies produce.

Banded Kukri *(Oligodon arnensis)*

Generally chestnut brown, and boldly banded with dark brown or black, this snake averages 12 inches but may grow to twice that length. On the head and neck it has black inverted 'V' markings. It is a nocturnal predator and during the day hides in cavities on the ground or in trees, its prey consisting of lizards and small rodents.

Checkered Keelback Watersnake *(Xenochropis piscator)*

Found along water-courses, keelbacks are generally between 18 inches and 3 feet long, but can grow much bigger. They have checkered markings on skin that varies from yellowish to very dark. They hunt fish, frogs and rodents.

Trinket Snake *(Elaphe helena)*

The trinket is a brownish snake with dark stripes, two on each side of the neck, and broad lateral bands running along the posterior part of the body. Averaging 2 to 3 feet long, they feed largely on rats and rest in cavities in the ground and among rocks.

Bronzeback Tree Snake *(Dendrelaphis tristis)*

This non-venomous snake is characterized by a broad bronze stripe running down the middle of its back, flanked with brown or black on the sides. Averaging over 3 feet long, it spends a lot of its time on trees, often jumping from branch to branch. Females are said to lay eggs in tree holes.

Other snakes reported in the park include the Indian egg-eater (*Elachistodon westormanni*), the common smooth water snake (*Enhydris enhydris*), Siebold's smooth water snake (*Enhydris sieboldi*), and the red-necked keel-back (*Rhabdophis subminiata*).

CROCODILES

Marsh Mugger *(Crocodylus palustris)*.
Nepali: magar—gohi

Crocodiles can be distinguished from alligators by the large tooth fourth from the front on each side of the lower jaw, which fits into a corresponding notch in the upper jaw (lip), revealing that tooth even when the mouth is closed. (In alligators the tooth lies buried in a socket.) The difference is best seen when a mugger is viewed from the side; the projecting tooth, together with the wavy outline of its mouth, gives it a rather nasty, smiling appearance. It is an endangered species and is found in low numbers in Nepal, India, Sri Lanka and Pakistan.

The mugger prefers to live in marshes and lakes, but is also seen in the rivers. Large specimens in Chitwan may reach 14 feet, but most of them are smaller. Though subsisting largely on fish and other aquatic animals, they are said to eat anything they can kill, capture or scavenge. Both in water and on land they are surprisingly agile — a fact belied by their favourite hunting tactic, which is to lie motionless for hours at a stretch on a bank near the water until they almost become part of the scenery: then, if some animal is unwary enough to wander within range, they react like lightning, seizing large mammals such as deer, dragging them into the water and drowning them. (In 1979 a man was killed by a mugger in the Rapti: he had been prodding the reptile with a stick, to see what it would do, when it suddenly went for him and pulled him into the river.)

Because of their very long palates, their internal nostrils open deep into the throat and can be closed with valves, enabling them to handle struggling prey beneath the surface without themselves inhaling water. With their huge, powerful jaws and sharp, gripping teeth (which are replaced as they are lost), they tear victims apart and swallow large chunks of flesh without chewing them. In Chitwan one was seen scavenging on a tiger kill, and at the approach of its rightful owner it dashed into the water. Another was seen with a large tortoise about 18 inches across between its jaws on the bank of an ox-bow lake. They also feed on human dead bodies

thrown into the Narayani and in this way maintain sanitation along the rivers.

Sometimes they travel considerable distances overland in search of food or while commuting from place to place, but they spend much of their time motionless, either in the water or on the bank, depending on the season of the year. Their movements are governed to some extent by the need to regulate their body temperature. In winter they bask in the sun for most of the day to bring their temperature up to a level at which their bodies can function fast and efficiently enough to catch prey. In summer they keep cool by lying in the water, often with their mouths gaping wide open so that they lose heat from the moist inner surfaces.

Not much is known about their breeding behaviour in Chitwan, but some knowledge has been gleaned from other sources. In the Madras Crocodile Bank, for instance, a large dominant male was seen to clap his jaws in the water as he chased and bit the smaller males as a prelude to his mating with up to five females.

Opinions vary about the age at which muggers attain sexual maturity. One school of thought says that it is not until they are six or seven years old; but recent research in India suggests that four captive males reached their presumed breeding size of about 5'6'' at the age of only two and a half. Two of these males mated frequently, at the age of three years eight months, and sizes of 5'7" and 6'7" respectively, with a female which had been attracted towards them and captured for that purpose. This indicates that size may be an important factor in inducing sexual maturity: similar observations have been recorded elsewhere.

In Chitwan the muggers' breeding period is not precisely known, but, judging from their hatching dates, it seems that late January to March are the most likely months for mating. They excavate nests up to 18 inches deep in raised sandbanks or in the earth. Clutch-size varies between six and thirty-six eggs, according to the size of the female. The incubation period depends upon the temperature of the nest and is therefore affected by the rains. Usually eggs take between two and three months to hatch. Females are known to guard their nests from a convenient distance. They return at intervals to inspect the site, but if the area is much disturbed they come back less frequently. The mother responds to the 'hatching calls' given by the unborn young from within the eggs by excavating the nest and leading the babies into water. Female Nile and Estuarine crocodiles have been known to carry their hatchlings in their gular pouches, and similar maternal behaviour was recorded for the mugger in 1978.

In Chitwan maximum hatching seems to take place in July. A hatchling was seen coming out of its egg and rushing into the water at Devi Tal in mid-July 1979. The mother had presumably taken fright at the approach of the domestic elephant, and disappeared with other babies (the nest had been properly excavated and the site was littered with egg shells). Around the same time of the year in 1981 a recently-excavated nest, with fresh tracks of the mother leading away towards the river, was seen near the old Rapti river. One winter a large female with several babies was seen in a drying pool, apparently feeding on fish stranded there.

Mortality among the young is very high. Although some nests hatch 90 per cent of their eggs, others are totally destroyed, and of the babies that do emerge a large proportion are killed in the first months by otters, storks, jackals, monitor lizards and other predators.

This fact, combined with a progressive reduction of good mugger habitat, has brought the population in Chitwan down to no more than seventy-five or a hundred, out of a total of between 2,000 and

3,000 in India as a whole (Sri Lanka is estimated to contain another 3,000).

In Chitwan, as elsewhere, ecological separation between the mugger and the gharial, or fish-eating crocodile, has been effectively achieved by the first living largely in lakes and marshes and the second exclusively in rivers. By doing this the two species have reduced competition for food, space and breeding grounds.

The Nile crocodile in Africa is known to feed selectively on predatory fish such as catfish, which themselves prey upon other fish, which in turn use lower food chains. This means that unless the crocodiles controlled their numbers, the catfish would take a heavy toll of prey species — that is, commercial fish. If this is true also for Chitwan, the importance of gharial and mugger in maintaining the ecological balance in the rivers and lakes cannot be overemphasised.

Gharial *(Gavialis gangeticus). Nepali: Gharial gohi.*

The gharial is so called because of the bulbous growth which large breeding males develop on the end of their snouts, and which resembles a *ghara* (Hindi for 'pitcher'), so that 'gharial' means 'one with the pitcher'. It is quite distinct from other crocodilians (crocodiles, alligators and caimans), and belongs to a separate family, *Gavialidae*, of which it is the only representative. It is the rarest of all crocodilians, found only in isolated pockets of the Ganges, the Brahmaputra and the Mohanadi river systems, with a world population of fewer than two hundred adults in the wild. The largest single concentration of these, numbering about fifty adults, survives in the Narayani river.

Large specimens exceeding 20 feet long have been known in the past, but those that we see in Chitwan today average 14-16 feet. They are almost exclusively fish-eating: their long, thin snouts are perfect weapons for snapping fish, which they catch by jerking their heads sideways. Other adaptations for hunting in water include a streamlined body, webbed hind feet, long and powerful tail laterally compressed into a fish-shape for propulsion, periscopic eyes, and valvular nostrils placed on top of the rostrum.

The breeding season opens in January/February when males are

seen with their harem of females on favourite spots along the river. One male was found violently splashing in the river for several seconds, to the accompaniment of hissing sounds, while others rested on the bank apparently unconcerned. Whether this was some kind of a sexual display was not known, but we strongly suspect territorial behaviour among males. One large male was seen with a harem of up to twelve females for many days in early March, 1979.

Gharials reach sexual maturity at six to ten years in the wild; females presumably earlier. Males become intolerant of other males during the breeding period, therefore larger older males probably monopolise most matings. On 4 March 1982, after some courtship behaviour in the water, a male mounted a female on the banks of the Narayani, their tails typically intertwined to facilitate coitus, and showed little concern about a boat floating by only 50 yards off. A mating was also recorded in late February 1978. Actual mating lasts only a short time. Before nesting (which in Chitwan usually happens in April) females disperse in search of a suitable site, perhaps within the male's territory. Because of the limited nesting areas available, many spots are used regularly, year after year. Raised sandbanks are preferred, in areas of minimal disturbance; the female digs a hole about 20 inches deep and lays between sixteen and sixty eggs, although larger clutches have been found. The nest is then covered with sand. Females generally stay a short distance from their nests but recently they seem to have given up guarding them in the face of increased human disturbance.

Many casualties are suffered even before the eggs hatch. Predators like otters and jackals take their toll, and local people steal eggs for their nutritional and purported medicinal values. Because of human activity near potential nesting sites, gharials may be obliged to lay eggs in less-than-ideal places, so that the nests are liable to be destroyed by the early floods. Increasing disturbance in certain localities may even deter them from breeding at all.

When the eggs do hatch — usually within seventy to ninety days, depending on the temperature in the nest — the mortality is astronomical. At birth the hatchlings are about a foot long, but very vulnerable, and it has been estimated that in the wild only one or two per cent survive to become adults.

By the late 1970s all these damaging factors had combined to produce a disastrous fall in the gharial population. For years nobody had seen any wild baby gharials in Chitwan, and several adults had been found dead. With no natural breeding success, and the adult stock declining steadily, the reptilian giants seemed threatened with extinction.

Fortunately in 1978 help came from the Frankfurt Zoological Society, which funded a rescue programme. Since protection alone was clearly not going to save the gharial, an artificial hatching and rearing centre was set up at Kasara, the park headquarters, some 12 miles east of Tiger Tops.

Once a nursery of rectangular cement tanks with sloping bottoms had been built, the first step was to collect eggs from nests that seemed precariously situated. The local fishermen, known as Boteys, were called in to help, since they knew all the sites, and were encouraged by small rewards. Well-sited nests were left intact, but eggs from the others were taken and reburied in artificial nests dug out of sandbanks on the river's edge.

When the hatchlings emerged, they were transferred to the tanks filled with river water and fed on a mixture of dead and live fish. Growth was good and mortality low. By the time they reached a length of 5 feet — between the ages of two and a half and three years — it was considered safe to release them into the rivers, for adult gharials have no natural predators, and are in general very shy of humans, although attacks on humans have been recorded in both India and Nepal. (Local people believe that the penis and rostral protuberance of males possess aphrodisiac qualities, for which they sometimes kill them.)

The first batch of fifty subadult gharials was released into the Narayani on 2 March 1981, by Sir Peter and Lady Scott. All were numbered and tagged, and ten of them were fitted with radio transmitters. The radio equipment had been given by the Smithsonian Institute of Washington DC, and additional funds for the reintroduction project had been provided by the International Trust for Nature Conservation. T. M. Maskey, then Senior Warden of the park, began the task of monitoring the young gharials' movements and collecting data on their ecology. Although similar hatching, reintroduction and research projects had been going on in India before the Chitwan programme began, this was the first time that radio-telemetry had been used on young gharials. Fifty more were released into the Narayani in the spring of 1982, and again ten were fitted with radios.

Only time will tell if this reintroduction scheme can succeed in re-establishing viable breeding populations in the wild, but already a good deal has been learnt — not least that patterns of population are greatly disrupted by the monsoon floods. Until the first monsoon after their release, most of the radio-gharials could be tracked in the river not far from the place of release, near Tiger Tops tented camp, but after the floods many disappeared. Some, we presume, went upstream, following the fish on which they were living and others were swept far downstream.

At the time of writing there are still two hundred and fifty young gharials in the research station, and the plan is to introduce them into other river systems in Nepal, such as those of the Kosi and the Karnali. If a rare and endangered animal is confined to diminishing ranges — as the gharial is — the best way to reduce the chance of random extinction is to expand its distribution as widely as possible.

LIZARDS

Monitors (*Varanidae*) are large lizards, with elongated bodies and strong limbs, and are confined to the Old World. The largest and the best-known of all is the Komodo Dragon (*Varanus komodoensis*) of Indonesia, which can grow to 10 feet or more. Monitors are powerful predators, with jaws adapted for swallowing large prey. Two species are listed in Chitwan.

Varanus monitor

These extremely agile lizards are 5 feet long, and they are found near grassland marshes and ponds and at the edge of forests. They hunt small mammals, birds and perhaps crocodiles' eggs, and also take carrion.

Varanus flavescens

Usually about 18 inches long, they are quite at home in trees and use hollows and holes in trees for nesting. They feed on smaller lizards, birds' eggs, nestlings and insects. One winter morning in 1983 an adult was found lying in the middle of the road immobilised by the low night temperature.

Agamidae

Calotes sp.

A very common Agamid lizard in Chitwan, the *Calotes* is usually seen in trees, but occasionally on the ground. It is highly active by day, hunting insects. It can grow to a length of 12 inches, and its scaly skin has spiny projections along the back. It can change its body colour depending on the temperature, and also during courtship displays. It develops conspicuous red patches on the sides of its neck and shoulders during the breeding season. At that time the males, which are more brightly coloured and larger than the females, are said to become highly territorial. A pair was seen mating on a tree in May. A female laid ten eggs in a small pit, 2 inches wide and the same deep, which she had dug in the ground, and later covered them.

There are doubtless several other Agamids and skinks (*Scincidae* — small, slim lizards) in the forests which have not been identified. A very rewarding project would be to collect and record all the lizards of the park.

Geckonidae

House Gecko *(Hemidactylus frentus)*

The house gecko is a common lizard which may be seen hunting insects on walls and ceilings at night. It gives distinctive loud clucking calls and grows to a length of about 6 inches. Its toes have highly-specialised swollen pads, each consisting of a multitude of extra-fine bristles which end in concave suction discs and enable it to move even on vertical glass panes.

TORTOISES

These long-lived, ancient reptiles (order: *Testudines,* also known as *Chelonia*) are characterised by their armour of bony carapace above and plastron below, both coated with horny scales called 'scutes'. They lay eggs in sand or earth, and their mouths, which are devoid of teeth, resemble birds' beaks. Very little is known about the life of these interesting creatures in the park, although many species are found in the marshes, lakes, rivers and forests, and vary considerably in size and form.

Also quite common in the park is the Indian starred tortoise (*Testudo elongata*). Three other species of tortoise are known to live here — *Trionyx gangeticus, Kachuga dhongoka,* and *K. Kachuga* — and species of *Chitra* and *Lissemys* are suspected of being present.

AMPHIBIANS

Frogs and toads collectively comprise *Anura,* the tail-less emphibians, which are widely preyed upon by birds such as storks and herons, and reptiles such as snakes. Their eggs — laid in large numbers in clusters or strings of jelly — are often eaten by fish. The amphibians themselves feed chiefly on invertebrates. Males call loudly during the breeding season, thereby attracting the females of their kind. During copulation, the male rides on the female's back by clasping her sides firmly, and as she produces her eggs he fertilises them externally, thereafter releasing her. The tadpoles that hatch out are at first aquatic vegetarians but eventually metamorphose into carnivorous adults that spend most of their time on land.

Frogs (*Ranidae*) have moist, slimy skins, pointed snouts and bulging eyes. They can leap well on their long hindlegs, the elongated toes of which are webbed, making them excellent swimmers. The loud mating calls of the males are a familiar sound during the monsoon, when a booming chorus of *or-or, or-or,* seems to resound from every side. Frogs (*Rana sp.*) are commonly found along rivers, lakes and wetlands.

Toads (*Bufonidae*), on the other hand, have warty skins, blunt heads and shorter hindlimbs, and inhabit drier areas. Their main defence is a poisonous milky juice which they can exude from their skins, mainly from the area behind each eye known as the parotid glands. Toads habitually feast on insects attracted to lamps and lights on summer and monsoon nights.

12 Invertebrates

Leeches *(Class: Hirudinae)*

Many visitors to Chitwan are nervous about the possibility of being bitten by leeches, but their fears are greatly exaggerated. It is not in the least painful to get a leech on your body — and in fact a bite is not usually noticed until the leech has dropped off and the wound bleeds. If one *is* found hanging on, it can easily be dislodged by applying salt.

Leeches are common in shaded areas of the park, especially in the grasslands, between June and November. Their tough, elastic bodies — normally just over an inch long when flaccid — are annulated, and vary in colour from light brown to black. At the back end is a vacuum sucker with which the creature grips its prey or host, and the mouth at the other end has sharp teeth for puncturing the skin.

A leech moves by repeatedly bringing one end of its body up to the other, making a quick succession of hoops. When it bites, it injects an anti-coagulant which prevents natural clotting of the blood, and in a short time it can suck enormous quantities, which it stores in its highly distensible crop. It was this outstanding ability as a blood-sucker that led to *Hirudo medicinalis* being widely used on human patients in the past.

Once a leech has had a meal, it can go without further food for many months. If humans are walking a path in Indian file, it is almost always the ones at the back who get bitten most, the leeches having been roused up by the passage of the first few feet.

In winter they are seldom seen, for they go underground and lie up; but during the monsoon tiny babies appear all over the place. Altogether some three hundred species are known around the world, and although most suck blood from mammals, reptiles and fish, others prey on invertebrates such as snails and worms.

Millipedes *(Class: Diplopoda)*

Millipedes are commonly found on the forest floor, where they feed on decaying vegetation. They do not have a thousand legs, as their name suggests: their cylindrical bodies are segmented, each segment having two pairs of legs, except that at the front, which has one pair, and the one at the back, which has none. Millipedes vary in size from very small to 4 inches or more in length. In defence many species secrete a disagreeable fluid from the sides of their body, and some curl up into a ball.

Centipedes *(Class: Chilopoda)*

These predators have flattened, segmented bodies, each segment bearing one pair of jointed legs, although the first pair is modified into claws. One species of *Scolopendra* found in Chitwan reaches a length of 12 inches, but most centipedes are much smaller. Their long legs enable them to run fast, and they kill prey such as insects and spiders by injecting poison with their teeth. Some species can give painful bites to humans, and the bitten part may remain swollen for several days.

Spiders *(Class: Arachnida; Order: Araneida)*

These interesting carnivores have eight legs and as many simple eyes. Largely insectivorous, they immobilise their prey by injecting venom via a pair of pincers. Digestive juices are then introduced into the body of their victim and the food thus partly dissolved is sucked in. Specialised abdominal spinnerets produce a liquid which in contact with air hardens to form silk. Many spiders weave webs to capture prey, and others such as wolf spiders and jumping spiders pounce on unwary prey. A particularly common spider in Chitwan weaves a characteristic web with an 'X' mark at the centre. On winter mornings the golden web spider can be seen weaving huge silk webs up to 15 feet across. Some gregarious spiders weave thick communal nests on bushes. In Chitwan the brown wood and the bird-eating spiders are among the largest, their leg-spans exceeding six inches. Interesting courtship displays have been reported, and during mating the male runs the risk of being eaten by his mate.

Arachnids such as spiders, scorpions, ticks and mites all have four pairs of legs, and the body is divided into cephalothorax (or head and chest) and abdomen.

Scorpions *(Order: Scorpionida)*

Scorpions are not often seen in Chitwan — which is perhaps just as well, for some species can give painful stings that may last up to a few days. The *prosoma* (or front part of the body) is covered by a carapace, and the abdomen (or *opisthosoma*) is made up of twelve segments, the last five being elongated into a tail, at the tip of which is a poisonous sting.

Venom from the sting paralyses and kills any prey that the scorpion captures with its claws: the victim is then torn apart by the jaws and eaten piecemeal. In courtship the pair 'dance' pincer-in-pincer, the male eventually guiding the female to his sperm sac, which he has dropped on the ground earlier, and often mating ends with the female eating her partner. If this seems tough on the male, it does make biological sense. By mating, the male has contributed his genes to heredity. Now, to raise his offspring, the female needs a lot of food and energy. High-class protein is available in the form of the male's body — so in sacrificing himself he is in fact helping to make sure that his genes are passed on to the next generation. Females give birth to live young which attach themselves to the mother's back and hitch-ride until they become independent after their first moult.

Ticks *(Order: Mestastigmata/Acarina)*

Ticks abound in the park, where they parasitise reptiles, birds and mammals, including man, and are carriers of many diseases. Their mouthparts are specialised for piercing, sucking and very firm attachment. The thorax and abdomen form a highly-distensible, extra-tough pouch, and they can engorge themselves with dozens of times their body-weight in blood. They are said to detect the presence of a host by the carbon dioxide which it exhales. They may remain lodged on a host for several days, and once full they drop off. Tick bites can be painful, and may lead to irritation and infection: if a tick is found *in situ*, the best remedy is to pull it off with pincers, making sure that the head comes away as well as the body.

Mites *(Order: Prostigmata/Acarida)*

Unlike ticks, mites parasitise plants as well as animals, and carry several diseases. Generally they resemble ticks in miniature and are found in all environments. In Chitwan the sinduri mite causes severe itching and irritation in humans during the monsoon.

Mosquitoes *(Order: Diptera; Family: Culicidae)*

Of the many species found in Chitwan, *Anopheles* and *Culex* are important in that the females are carriers of malaria and encephalitis respectively. Mosquitoes are common in the park from April to November, July to September being the worst months. Not all of them suck blood; however, gravid females of many species do need human and vertebrate blood. All males and many females feed on plant-sap and nectar. Eggs are usually laid in stagnant water, and the larvae that emerge are aquatic, feeding on microscopic plants and animals and breathing via a pair of spiracles that pierce the water surface. The larval stages pass on to become pupae, which in turn become adults. Males and females have different frequencies of wing-vibrations, and therefore produce sounds of different pitch. A cheap, finger-sized electronic gadget has recently proved an effective defence against bites. By posing as males, which pregnant females avoid, the owners of such gadgets render themselves immune — for females cannot apparently distinguish between natural and artificially-produced male sounds.

Termites *(Order: Isoptera)*

Termites are social insects that live in colonies underground or in wood and are notorious for the damage they do to timber, stationery and fabrics. Colonies build mounds of different shapes and sizes, and some species grow fungi for food in their interior galleries. Termites feed mainly on cellulose, the digestion of which is facilitated by symbiotic intestinal bacteria.

Each colony is divided into the workers and soldiers, which are sterile and wingless, and the reproductives, which grow wings and swarm at certain times of the year to mate and form new colonies. The original pair become the king and the queen, the latter capable of producing millions of eggs in her life that may span a dozen years or more. In Chitwan most swarming takes place just before the monsoons. Usually the winged termites come out after a shower, and the air is suddenly full of their swarms. Sometimes one sees the ground erupt, in a totally unexpected place, and thousands burst out into the light.

Termite mounds, with their pale, fluted sides and irregular pinnacles rising to a height of 6 or 8 feet, are a familiar sight in the sal forest; they are intricate structures, with a very effective system of ventilation. The sloth bear specialises in feeding on their colonies, thus helping to control their numbers. Termites are also called white ants, although they are not in fact closely related to ants. They are rich in protein, and some tribals in India cook and eat them.

Fireflies *(Order: Coleoptera; Family: Lampyridae)*

Fireflies are tiny beetles, and since the females of many species resemble larvae, they are also called glow-worms. In Chitwan the common firefly's body is warningly coloured in bright orange and black, but the intermittent glow which it gives off is greenish. Often, on summer nights, whole colonies of them may be seen in the treetops, flashing in synchrony.

The lighting is used for courtship display: each species has a particular glow, peculiar to itself. The illumination is produced by specialised glands in the terminal segments of the abdomen; these contain luciferin, which, in the presence of air and an enzyme called luciferase, generates light. The duration of each signal, and the intervals between, can be controlled by the insect, regulating the amount of air which comes into contact with the luciferin.

Antlions *(Family: Myrmeleontidae)*

In the park the sandy forest paths are dotted with funnel-shaped pitfalls, usually an inch or two across, made by the predaceous larvae of the antlion. The larva stays at the bottom of the funnel with only its jaws showing. As soon as an ant or other insect falls into the trap, it flicks sand, making escape difficult, and having secured the victim sinks further into the sand. However, many antlion larvae do not make traps: they pupate in the sand, and the adults that emerge resemble dragonflies and damselflies.

Stick Insects *(Order: Phasmida)*

This large group of insects offers a fascinating example of creatures that have adapted to resemble their background. As their name suggests, they have slender bodies up to 8 inches long, usually green or brown, and blend so well with twigs and branches that they look like part of the environment. Their habit of remaining motionless at the first sign of danger, or dropping down as if lifeless when handled, reinforces the deception. Most lack wings, and in those that do possess them only the hindwings are well developed, the forewings being reduced. Since they feed on vegetation, they hardly need to move. Many species are said to reproduce parthenogenetically — that is, without the help of a male.

Close relatives are the leaf insects, which are leaf-like in appearance, with flattened body and limbs. Like the stick insects, they live on plants and trees and feed on leaves. These strange animals are especially common in the grassland during the monsoon.

Praying Mantises *(Order: Dictyoptera)*

Their name is derived from their habit of resting with their forelegs folded and held in front of them, as if in prayer. Mantises are carnivores and prey on other insects. After mating, the female, which is larger and up to 4 inches long, often feeds on her mate, and eggs are laid in a frothy mass that solidifies rapidly.

Cicadas *(Order: Homoptera; Family Cicadidae)*

Cicadas are more often heard than seen, and usually stay on trees where they feed on sap. The males produce their distinctive loud monotone by vibrating a membrane on each side of the abdomen, and the sound — designed to attract mates — differs from species to species. Perhaps the most renowned of them all are the periodical cicadas found in the USA, which have thirteen- and seventeen- year life cycles.

Ants *(Order: Hymenoptera; Family: Formicidae)*

Ants live in colonies, usually started by a fertilised female known as the queen. The workers — all sterile females without wings — procure food, build the nest and protect it, and take care of the young and the queen. At certain times of the year the queen produces fertilised offspring of both sexes that grow wings and swarm. Pairs mate, the males soon die, and those females that survive start new colonies.

In Chitwan most ants live in the ground, but the black tree ants make a tough, spherical nest on a horizontal branch, and the red ants glue several leaves together, usually high up in a tree; although they are very sour in taste, local people sometimes eat them. Some ants such as the rotey (red with black waists) can sting, causing much itching.

Honey bees *(Family: Apidae)*

Honey bees are social insects, and have been exploited by man for honey and wax over thousands of years. They live in large, highly-sophisticated colonies, consisting of a fertile female — the queen — thousands of sterile females, or workers, and some males, or drones, that appear from time to time. The queen, who may live for several years, lays eggs, and her offspring from the larva stage on are fed on 'royal jelly', a specially-enriched food.

The workers produce wax with which they construct the combs, take care of the young, defend their colonies (after stinging they die), and make honey from nectar which they collect from flowers, together with pollen grains. The honey, besides being highly nutritious, is much valued for its medicinal qualities. At certain times a queen and her workers swarm to form new colonies. Apart from their economic importance to man, bees are also valuable for the pollination of plants.

The common honey bee in Chitwan is the large *Apis dorsata*, which builds big combs on trees and rock overhangs. Several dozen combs have often been reported in a single kapok tree. The smaller *Apis indica* is also found in the forest, and it is commonly domesticated and maintained in wooden hives by villagers.

Most of the honey is made in spring and summer, when the majority of trees and plants are in flower. Sloth bears are particularly fond of honey, and readily climb trees to feed on it. They are protected against stings by their shaggy coats, but their muzzles seem to have some other form of defence. Villagers enter the park illegally to forage for honey, and show great intrepidity in smoking out and robbing the nests. Honey-gatherers are frequently stung in the process — and multiple stings can be dangerous. Even one sting is painful and causes local swelling, but for anyone hypersensitive to bee poison the effect can be positively alarming.

13   Predator-prey relations

For a naturalist — and indeed for a visitor — one of the most fascinating features of Chitwan is the way in which every piece of the ecological jig-saw interlocks. With the exception of the tiger — the master predator — and of the rhino and elephant, which have grown impregnably large, every animal is potential prey — and therefore potential food — for some other creature. Similarly, the grasses, plants and trees all offer food to various species, and the disposition of the different kinds of vegetation has a direct influence on where the various kinds of animals live. The herbivores, in particular, have strong habitat-preferences.

The hog deer restricts itself to the grassland, and, being an exclusive grazer, is seldom found outside that habitat: it favours the short grassland especially. The rhino is predominantly a grazer, but supplements its diet with browse in the forests and aquatic plants from swamps and lakes. Unlike the hog deer, which feeds only on short grass and tender shoots, the rhino uses both short and tall coarse grasses.

The chital are mixed feeders, inhabiting short grasslands as well as lowland forests. Though primarily animals of open country, they have adapted well to the denser vegetation characteristic of Chitwan. But they keep out of the sloping highland forests and tall grasslands. The small barking deer browse a lot on the forest floor and also feed on shoots at the edge of grassland. The sambar, essentially browsers, prefer the dense sal forest and mature riverine forests, but also do some grazing in the open.

By offering such a variety of habitats, the existing mosaic of vegetation meets the food requirements of most ungulates. For example, during the gradual progression from grassland to forest, the hog deer is affiliated with the early stages of succession, the rhino with the early to intermediate stages, the chital with the intermediate stages, and the sambar and barking deer with the late intermediate stages. In other words, through specialisation the ungulates make optimal use of food resources.

Two other large herbivores — the wild buffalo and the swamp deer — once fitted into this pattern. Both animals of marshes and wetlands interspersed with short and tall grasslands, they were driven out by the mass of human settlers who invaded Chitwan in the 1950s and took over most of their habitat along the Rapti river. Alteration and loss of habitat, competition from domestic livestock and the possible introduction of diseases are more than enough to account for their extinction. The wild elephants, which were still common in eastern Chitwan thirty years ago, inhabited the hill forests, which satisfied their partiality for bamboo. Being mainly grazers, they presumably made regular forays into the grasslands for the tall, lush species they savour. But then they too disappeared from the valley; only a few remain on the southern slopes of the Churia hills near Amnwa.

The rugged terrain of the Siwalik hills to the south provides a home for the mighty gaur, who normally live high up, but venture down to the plains to take advantage of the new growth after the early grass fires of January. During the dry winter months food and water become scarce on the hills, and the fires of March and April finish off what little forage remains there. During that period the gaur feast on the nutritious shoots that abound on the plains, and stay there until May, when the pre-monsoon showers begin to stimulate regeneration in the hills. Then the herds move up again, and stay high for the rest of the year.

The ever-elusive serow — the ungainly goat-antelopes — make a living on the highest crestlines of the hills. The wild boar, on the other hand, are versatile feeders and are therefore widespread throughout the park. Even more widespread are the ubiquitous rats and mice. The hares inhabit the grasslands, and the porcupines are mainly forest-dwellers.

Many of the park's resources, in the form of foliage, flowers and fruit, grow high up in the trees, out of reach of most land-dwelling mammals. Some creatures, however, have evolved ways of using the harvest overhead. Elephants and rhinos, for instance, adopt heavyweight tactics and push over small trees so that they can feed on the tops. Monkeys and squirrels, in contrast, have developed the ability to climb.

The langurs feed on the treetops, moving from tree to tree and pruning as they go, without seriously damaging any single tree. At first glance they may seem rather wasteful feeders, but the litter they drop is readily eaten by deer, who usually follow them on the forest floor. Rhesus macaques are also tree-climbers, but find their food on the ground as well. Squirrels and flying squirrels lead arboreal lives. One branch of mammals — the bats — adopted a totally different means of locomotion and became fliers. Thus they compete for the same resources as birds — fruit, nectar and insects — but reduce competition by foraging mainly at night.

Altogether, it is clear that the herbivores of Chitwan are making (and always *have* made) the best possible use of food resources through niche-separation. However, it should not be forgotten that today at least thirty-eight domesticated elephants are maintained in the park, and that thousands of domestic livestock graze illegally within its boundaries, especially along the periphery.

The herbivores tend to live singly or in small, scattered groups, for two reasons — efficient feeding and defence. In areas of close, tall cover sufficient forage is not available for a large number of animals within a small range, and to move about in big groups would make them both more conspicuous and more vulnerable to attack. Herds are therefore usually small, and since each animal is more or less a law unto itself, every one is wary and shy, always on the alert, employing its faculties of smell, hearing and sight to detect and avoid predators. Since visibility is often severely limited, the herbivores' eyes are only moderate, but they have extra-sharp noses and ears.

In open ground, however, they can afford to form larger groups. Chital herds over a hundred-strong and hog deer herds of ten to twelve animals are often seen in recently-burned areas. The hog deer also tend to group together on open river banks, but scatter as soon as they enter cover. Gaur herds of ten to twenty animals, so common in the plains, presumably break up into smaller units on the hills (humans are rarely there to observe them). All the animals are instinctively responding to their inbuilt defence mechanisms: they seem to realise that living in scattered parties in close cover increases their chances of survival, but that when cover is minimal it is safer to congregate.

In open areas such as burned grasslands food is relatively

plentiful, so many animals can feed together, and by forming large groups they also reap the benefits of group vigilance (that many pairs of eyes and ears and nostrils on the alert) which renders them less vulnerable to attack. Stalking predators are put at a further disadvantage by the loss of cover so vital for a close approach.

Escape from predation may be effected by several other means. When pursued by wild dogs, sambar and chital run into water. If a tiger or leopard is spotted on the move, the jungle rings with the alarm calls of deer, langurs and peafowl. Prey animals feed mainly in the safety of darkness (although in summer another reason for coming out at night is to avoid the midday heat).

Herbivores need large quantities of low-calorie food, and if all of it had to be chewed properly before being swallowed, they would be gathering food for longer hours, exposing themselves to more danger. Evolution has, however, given them an extra pouch, in which they store hurriedly-collected food, to be masticated in safety. Langurs have a similar pouch, but the rhesus do not. Instead, they have distensible cheek pouches for the same purpose. It is interesting that the invulnerable elephants and rhinos do not have such pouches and feed for fifteen hours or more each day.

The deer have evolved a repertoire of visual, auditory and olfactory signals which serve to warn their fellows and others of danger. The association between chital and langur, and between chital and hog deer and rhesus, may benefit both parties: monkeys have acute vision, and the deer have acute hearing and smell, making the combination less vulnerable.

Most animals try to avoid capture by escaping detection and by running away. No doubt that is usually the best thing to do — to get away from the predator as soon as possible. Yet some creatures seem to decide that attack is the best form of defence. A lone wild boar or a couple of them may attack a tiger or a leopard and come off better. A female rhino may attack and chase off a tiger while defending her young. A large gaur bull may be more than a match for a tiger, and a group of gaur even more so.

There are even more subtle ways of guarding against enemies. The long, piercing quills of a porcupine can and do cause fatalities among leopards and tigers. The stink glands of civets and the scales of the pangolin are both efficient protective devices (civets are garishly coloured to warn potential predators of the consequences).

The rhino and the elephant have become so large that adults are virtually immune to any predator. These and other defences evolved by prey are what Schaller describes as 'anti-predator patterns, some morphological and physiological in nature and others behavioural, but all directly or indirectly designed to reduce the chance of the animals being eaten'. As Schaller also points out, no species can have a perfect defence against predators, 'for selection works in such a way that any increase in the efficiency of the escape pattern brings about a refinement in the method of attack by the predators'. Animals cannot always be defending themselves; it would be impractical, uneconomical and self-defeating. They have to eat, drink, rest, fight and breed — and in any of these pursuits they expose themselves to attack.

The way in which Chitwan's dense forests favour stalking predators rather than coursing ones is shown by the relative numbers of species present:

STALKERS	COURSERS
1. Tiger	1. Wild dog
2. Leopard	2. Golden jackal
3. Fishing cat	3. Fox (only at or outside
4. Marbled cat (suspect)	park's edge)
5. Jungle cat	
6. Leopard cat	

Jackals are found in some numbers, and prey on small mammals, birds and reptiles, but wild dogs and foxes are both very scarce. The group-hunting wild dogs are efficient killers: they run their quarry down after a long chase, singling out the slow and weak, whose fate is sealed by the relentless and tireless pursuit. Their rate of success is high, and they kill many of the same species as the tiger, but there are so few of them in Chitwan that their impact on prey populations is small. A few deer are also taken by crocodiles and pythons, but both these feed mostly on smaller creatures.

It is the tiger and leopard which prey mainly on the medium-sized ungulates, from sambar down to muntjac. Tigers and leopards do not mix well; leopards, being smaller and less powerful, usually move out of an area well stocked with tigers. In Chitwan, however, there are a fair number of them, and there is some ecological separation between the two species. In other words, the tigers concentrate on larger animals and the leopards on smaller ones.

Competition between the two is thus reduced; there is still some prey overlap, but this is to some extent offset by the large amount of prey available. Because of the tigers' dominance, the leopards maintain a low profile, and clashes are kept to a minimum, partly by the leopards' vigilance, partly by poor visibility. Leopards also seek refuge from tigers by climbing trees. They appear to be more numerous along the park's periphery than in the prime areas of the interior, but this is perhaps more from force of circumstance than from choice.

For this close environment, with its medium-sized prey, the tiger has adopted the most efficient hunting technique: a single-handed attack by stalk and ambush. Group hunting would be unproductive and uneconomical. In thick cover the cohesion of a pack can be maintained only by vocal contact, and this betrays the hunters' presence. The location of shy and scattered prey is best done by one guerrilla operating alone.

The absence of serious rivals enables tigers to make the fullest use of each kill by feeding off it for several days. Although largely opportunistic, they have to make a kill at least every week or so, and this perhaps increases their hunting success in another way: if all tigers were to hunt daily, the prey would either move out or increase its vigilance to such a degree that a kill would be even harder to bring off.

It would be wrong, however, to assume that solitary tigers find it easy to capture prey; most of their hunts undoubtedly end in failure (one estimate suggests that only one hunt in twenty succeeds). Just as the tiger has evolved to become a professional hunter, so the prey species have evolved to become professionals at not being eaten. Nonetheless, all things considered, in a closed environment such as Chitwan the solitary hunting strategy of the tiger shows a high degree of evolutionary adaptation, compared with the impractical and energy-inefficient communal manoeuvres of animals like wild dogs or lions.

The leopard is another solitary hunter, with a propensity for smaller ungulates weighing from 60 to 120 lbs. The pressure on these, however, is somewhat offset by the fact that the leopard also takes langurs, rhesus monkeys and peafowl, which the tiger usually leaves alone. No one knows how many leopards there are in the park, but their predation must contribute to the overall figure of standing-crop removal in no small way.

In 1981 the American biologist Melvin Sunquist made some calculations on the amount of live prey eaten annually by tigers in Chitwan. He estimated the daily food requirements of a female to be 11-13 lbs, and of a male 13-15 lbs. Assuming that 30 per cent of each carcass is inedible, and that some meat is lost to scavengers (including humans) and through disturbance, he estimated annual requirements to be 5,700-7,200 lbs for a female and 6,800-8,100 lbs for a male. At the start of 1976, the tiger population was reckoned at three adult males, twelve adult females and fourteen young (two subadult males, two subadult females, six large young and four small cubs). Basing his calculations on the assumed food intake by the different age-classes, he came up with a nutritional equivalent of five adult males and eighteen adult females for the park (area then 210 square miles). Using Seidensticker's and Tamang's estimates for the density of wild ungulates, he calculated the crude biomass or live weight of prey available to tigers as being between 6,990 and 11,100 lbs per square mile, or from 1,462,470 to 2,328,973 lbs for the park as a whole.

If the tigers needed 143,000-176,000 lbs of prey in 1976, they took off 8-10 per cent of the standing crop. These calculations do not include predation on domestic livestock, which contributes a large amount to the tigers' diet in some areas. This being so, the tigers probably remove less than 8-10 per cent of the available live weight of prey. But if one includes the energy requirements of other predators in Chitwan as well, the total cull probably resembles the 9-10 per cent removal by lions, hyenas and other predators in the Serengeti computed by Schaller.

K. M. Tamang, writing in 1979, produced a lower estimate. Assuming that a tiger needs 15 lbs of meat a day, and again that 30 per cent of the carcass is inedible, he calculated that the thirty tigers reckoned to live in the park (area then 360 square miles) removed about 6.2 per cent of the standing crop biomass (excluding rhino, gaur and domestic livestock).

Both these sets of figures are for the park as a whole, and no distinction is made, as far as prey biomass is concerned, for the sal forest — although chital, a major prey item, live only in the lower sal forest. A very large proportion of the sal forest is hill country devoid of chital, but may contain higher densities of sambar, wild boar and muntjac. Nevertheless, it is unlikely that the upper sal forest carries the same biomass as the lower sal. Moreover, it appears that because of the broken, hilly terrain, prey are much less vulnerable in the upper sal than in the lower areas and the plains.

Small wonder that the tiger uses the low ground most heavily: not only are the density and biomass of prey highest there, but the animals are easier to catch. Most of the cropping therefore takes place in the lower sal and floodplain belt of habitats, which comprise only a fraction of the land in Chitwan. The rest of the park seems to act as a reservoir which constantly replenishes stock as it is removed.

How great is the pressure exerted by tigers on prey in prime habitats? In April 1982, four adult females, one adult male, two subadult females, one subadult male and two cubs born the previous November occupied about 40 square miles of prime habitat in western Chitwan between Tamar Tal and Ledaghat. The ratio of riverine forest and grassland to lower sal forest was about 7:3. According to Tamang's estimates the area must have contained some 552,000 lbs of prey. Using Sunquist's estimates of annual food requirements, one can calculate that the resident tigers removed 55,000-68,000 lbs of prey, or 9-11 per cent of the standing crop.

But the situation can change appreciably in years when resident females have large dependent cubs. For example, in June 1980, when there were seven large dependent cubs in roughly the same 40-square-mile area, the percentage removed by the total equivalent of two males and nine females probably went up from 9-11 per cent to between 11 and 14 per cent.

All these estimates exclude rhino, gaur and domestic livestock. These last form a considerable portion of the tigers' diet along the park's periphery and also near Tiger Tops, where the buffalo calves staked out as bait for nine months of the year are taken with some regularity. This readily-available buffer of alternate prey appears to help support large dependent cubs and subadult transients.

1980 seems to have been a year of unusually high tiger density, and in the area in question the stress on prey species may have reached its highest possible limits. Thereafter the non-resident tigers apparently spread out, perhaps adjusting their own numbers to match the natural prey supply.

Another interesting exercise is to compare the ratio of predator-weight to prey-weight with figures computed in other environments. Sunquist estimated 1 lb of tiger for between 390 and 630 lbs of prey (excluding rhino, gaur and domestic stock). This proved a very low ratio compared with those quoted by Schaller for various areas in Africa: about 1:250-300 in the Serengeti, 1:174 in Manyara, and 1:100 in the Ngorongoro Crater, Nairobi Park and Kruger Park.

The impact of predation on the numbers of prey can never be expected to be constant; it changes seasonally and from year to year, and also from species to species. During the grass-burning season, when hog deer and chital become less vulnerable because of the benefits of group vigilance and lack of cover, hunting of sambar and wild boar presumably increases. But when the grass is regrown, the pressure shifts again to the grassland and riverine forest species.

When an unknown disease reduced wild boar numbers severely in 1974, it seems that pressure on the sambar may have increased. Different animals react in different ways if predation on them becomes exceptionally heavy. Animals such as wild boar, with a high reproductive potential and widespread distribution, can probably withstand greater pressure than others. The versatile nature of the chital and the large habitat-range of the sambar also render them capable to tolerating increased predation, at least temporarily, without their rate of reproduction being seriously impaired.

And yet in the long run, in spite of so many variable factors, predation probably does have a stabilising effect on prey populations. Schaller noted that in Kanha National Park, in Central India, which in some ways resembles Chitwan except that it is a rather drier and more open environment, tiger predation 'has a strong depressive influence on the number of wild hoofed animals', but also that predator and prey populations are by and large self-limiting.

It must, however, be borne in mind that a predator may affect its prey differently from area to area, depending on a variety of other ecological conditions. According to Tamang, 'tiger predation alone is not limiting or adversely affecting its prey populations' in Chitwan. Sunquist holds a similar view: 'The high carrying capacity of the floodplains, combined with the multiple prey base, makes it unlikely that predation alone could have a long-term limiting effect on ungulate populations . . .'

All the evidence suggests that predation may be one important agency controlling population levels, but that other factors such as disease, intra-specific competition and habitat-condition act simultaneously to keep numbers within the threshhold of an area's carrying capacity.

What seems abundantly clear is that if the maximum number of predators is to be maintained, the park must be so managed as to increase its capacity for carrying the ungulates on which the predators live. Large tracts on the higher floodplains may have to be opened up in patches by physically clearing the tall grass and forest to create short-grass pastures on which greater concentrations of hoofed animals can graze. All remaining forests must be protected to act as buffer areas for absorbing animals which cannot find space in the park. The vigour of the predators is reflected in the vitality of their prey: it is constant hunting pressure that keeps the prey population going.

14 Tracks and signs of mammals

Animals that live in thick jungles are always difficult to spot.
Despite the great variety of mammals found in the park — over fifty
species — one is constantly surprised at how few are seen apart
from the relatively common rhinos, deer, pigs and monkeys. In fact
several of us who have had the singular opportunity of living in
Chitwan for several years have yet to see many of them. Much
depends upon chance; a visitor may see a tiger in broad daylight on
his first day in the park, a sight denied others for many years. Very
little is known about bats and rats, two unattractive yet important
groups in the ecology of the area.

Visibility is generally poor because of the dense vegetation, and
most mammals are nocturnal and shy — factors hardly conducive
to easy or good sightings. In these conditions the fact that an animal
is seldom seen does not necessarily mean that it is rare. The serow
is hardly ever sighted, mainly because it inhabits such remote and
inaccessible terrain. Ratels, or honey-badgers, have never actually
been seen in Chitwan. Their presence in the park was discovered
accidentally in 1980 when a pair of them took their own photograph
by treading on the pressure-plate of a camera set in the jungle by
Dr McDougal to obtain pictures of tigers.

Since it is so hard to see the great majority of Chitwan's mammals,
one must fall back on indirect techniques to identify and study
them. By observing their spoor, scats, scrapes, scratchings, shelters
and other signs, including scent and sound, the field naturalist
opens up new and fascinating vistas of detection work.

The most obvious animal signs are tracks. Tracking is an ancient
art used for centuries by man as a hunter and more recently in the
study of natural history. Many aboriginal tribes are well known for
their remarkable understanding of animal tracks. Trained *shikaris*
in Nepal are experts in this field, and the skill with which they
interpret pug-marks, hoof-prints and other scarcely-visible traces is

incredible. These *shikaris* are indispensable to any tiger darting operation today; to find an anaesthetised tiger they have to track it through thick grasslands in which visibility is only a few feet, relying on the scantiest signs — a twig broken, a patch of leaves disturbed, a tuft of grass pressed down but gradually springing back into its original attitude.

Open river banks, paths, trails and earth roads are ideal places to look for tracks — the usual signatures that animals inevitably leave on the ground as they move. Yet it can be most confusing, often impossible, even for the specialist to decide with certainty to which animal a particular set of tracks belongs. The study of tracks, however, can be refined to a high degree of sophistication: different individuals of the same species can be reliably identified by recording the idiosyncracies of their spoor. This has been done, with conspicuous success, by Dr Chuck McDougal for the tigers of western Chitwan; but such detailed study is only possible with large territorial mammals which occur in low densities.

Good tracks, with all the features clearly spelled out, are not always found: both size and shape can be distorted by the texture of the ground and the speed of locomotion. On soft earth or loose sand or in mud the size of tracks is exaggerated, as the surface yields under the animal's weight; whereas on hard ground the contours are more faithfully reproduced. Also, on soft ground or when the animal is moving fast, its feet spread for proper support. So, if an animal is running on sand its tracks are unusually large.

As a general rule, forefoot tracks are broader and larger than those of the hindfoot, except, for instance, among rodents, where the reverse is usually true. Young animals have compact toes, which become splayed out as they grow older. Deformities may also creep in with age. Usually females have smaller footprints than males. The fore and hindfeet may have different numbers of toes. One is amazed how the same individual can make quite different imprints as it moves over varying types of ground.

In deer, only two toes normally touch the ground, forefoot tracks being splayed out, while those of the hindfoot tend to be compact. The dew claws, growing higher up on the back of the leg, touch down only on soft ground or when the animal is bounding. Track sizes of different deer species overlap, making positive identification difficult. For example, a young sambar stag or subadult hind may have tracks about the same size as those of chital, although the latter usually have narrower and more elongated hoofs. Tracks of adults, however, may be accurately recognized with practice.

Wild boar have elongated dew claws which usually leave impressions, but unlike those of deer, which lie behind the two hoofs in the same line, the dew claws of pigs are set further out.

Gaur tracks resemble those of domestic cattle but are larger. Rhinos have large pads with three distinct toes on each foot; they also sometimes indulge in foot dragging, a habit associated with reproduction, which leaves tell-tale skidmarks. Elephants have very large pads with rather indistinct toe marks. Their front feet are circular, with five toes, and their hindfeet elongated, with four toes. I am often amazed by the certainty with which a *phanit* can recognize the tracks of his own elephant. Sometimes one of the park's trained elephants escapes at night and disappears into the jungle; but invariably by morning the *phanit* has tracked it and brought it home.

Cats have three-lobed main pads with four toes. Because their claws are retractile, they never leave claw-marks unless their feet are deformed or if they are excited.

Canids have relatively small pads, with four large toes, and leave claw marks. The prints of wild dogs are larger, squarer and more compact than the elongated ones of jackals and foxes, which have the two middle toes set forwards, leaving a large gap between those toes and the main pad. The claw marks of fox and jackal are sharp, but those of wild dogs quite blunt.

Hyenas have compact, rather irregular tracks like those of a dog, with uneven pads and four toes ending in thick, blunt claws. The most distinctive feature is that their forefeet are considerably larger than their hindfeet. Sloth bears have broad pads with five toes ending in long claws, longer in the forefoot. Usually only the front part of the sole of the forefoot touches the ground, so that no heel print is normally visible, but the hindfoot treads with its entire sole, leaving a mark like a caricature of a human footprint.

The yellow-throated marten has a crescent-shaped pad with five spreading toes and non-retractile claws. The forefoot track usually shows the imprint of a small pad behind the main pad.

The otter has five webbed toes with claws, details of which show clearly in a sharp print on mud. The hindfoot often shows the entire sole, and is longer than the forefoot.

Both the small and large Indian civets have small, compact feet and walk on four toes (*digitigrade*), with semi-retractile claws. The spotted linsang also has four toes, but completely retractile claws like those of cats. The tree-climbing palm civet has semi-plantigrade (front part of sole on ground) locomotion and treads on broad, hairy sole pads with five-clawed toes.

Mongooses have plantigrade (complete sole on ground) locomotion, with five splayed-out toes ending in non-retractile long claws; most forefoot tracks show only four toes.

Porcupines usually tread on their entire soles and leave impressions of four toes on each foot. The fifth toe of the hindfoot is visible only on clear prints.

Because of their very hairy soles, rufous-tailed hares make indistinct prints, although their claws leave sharp marks. They have four toes in the hindfoot and five in the forefoot but usually only four show (inner toe may be missing) in tracks. Hindfoot tracks are longer.

The langurs have longer hands and feet than rhesus macaques, but their thumbs are shorter. The toes of their feet have become long fingers: the big toe functions like a thumb and is opposable to the other toes.

No one should expect to be able to identify all the tracks he or she sees; even specialists have headaches trying to decipher many, especially those made by the smaller mammals. Tracks in the field may appear quite different from those shown here, although all the drawings were traced from real prints. The tracings were made from tracks on different kinds of surface, so there may be considerable variation in size, and they should be taken as approximates only. (Hard, flat ground with a thin layer of dust or mud, or a slightly receptive surface, is an ideal medium for realistic tracks.) A stay at Tiger Tops can become a most rewarding experience if the visitor takes a walk along river beds and paths and tries to identify the tracks left by animals in their passage.

An early-morning foray, made in the company of a trained *shikari*, may uncover many of the night's secrets. What, for instance, was the tigress doing when she came along this path during her nocturnal perambulations? Here she was walking steadily: her long, pointed toes identify her clearly as Chuchchi, one of the animals fitted with a collar-radio during the Smithsonian project. Here she sat down to listen: the marks of her haunches are pressed into the dust. Here she sprayed a jamun tree as she passed, advertising her presence: even to the blunt human nose the thick, sharp, musky scent can be picked up from a distance of several feet . . . Such observations, made regularly over a long period, build up a great deal of valuable information about the behaviour and ecology of the elusive big cats.

Many animals tend to use fixed trails, at least partly, and in time their routes form a well-established network of highways that criss-cross the forest floor and the otherwise impenetrable grassland. In areas of thick cover such fixed trails become familiar, safe and noiseless routes to travel, free of pits, bogs and other obstacles. They also furnish easy shortcuts to sources of food, as well as escape from predators. Rhinos frequently use their own paths and often start new ones by crashing through dense grass or undergrowth. In the hilly country of the park's interior, mammals' paths offer humans the best means of negotiating difficult terrain. Tigers and leopards use these paths as well, and presumably waylay or stalk and ambush unwary prey along them.

Besides leaving tracks, animals betray their presence in many different ways, and only a few obvious examples are given here. Langurs, as they feed from tree to tree, litter the ground with leaves in their wake. If parts of the forest floor are ploughed up, it is a sure sign that pigs have been rootling for food. Sloth bears dismantle and open up the bases of termite mounds for their pulpy occupants. They commonly dig large holes in search of food, a habit also shared by the ratel. Bears and leopards leave claw marks on the trees that they climb and scratch. Tigers habitually claw trees with their forefeet by standing upright against the trunk on their hindlegs. They seem to favour particular trees, which eventually become heavily scarred. Often fragments of their claws remain embedded in the bark, together with tufts of their fur. Some experts think that tigers rake their claws to clean and sharpen them, but others consider it a form of marking. These tiger trees are nearly always sprayed with scent as well.

One such tree — a kapok — stands near the path leading from Tiger Tops to the tented camp. Tigers frequently spray the trunk, and a thick horizontal branch about 6 feet off the ground is deeply-scored with claw marks on either side, showing that they often stand on their hindlegs and rake downwards with both forepaws at once.

Since this looked an excellent site at which to photograph tigers performing one of their natural functions, a camera with an infra-red trigger device was set up: the beam was aligned along one side of the horizontal branch, so that if a tiger interrupted the beam by clawing at the bark, a flashlight picture would be taken automatically. Several times hopes were raised when it was found that exposures had been taken during the night, but every film proved blank, the camera having been set off by a rain-drop, an insect or a falling leaf. At last a nocturnal rambler *was* photographed, but it proved to be only a sloth bear, sniffing inquisitively at the tigers' tree.

Tracks apart, the most characteristic signs left by deer are those made by the males during the rut. Their vigorous assault on the environment may be regarded as a form of redirected aggression, and the disturbance and damage they cause act as visual and scent signals to others.

Chital and sambar stags paw the ground with their forelegs, the cloven hooves making distinct scrape marks. Large, circular, bare patches of ground about a yard in diameter, underneath a tree, indicate the 'preaching' of males, who stand on their hindlegs and trample the soil while rubbing their heads among the foliage of a low branch. These bare areas are made by repeated preaching, and several stags may use the same spot. Another peculiar habit among deer is tree-fraying. When the new antlers stop growing, the covering of highly-vascularised tissue called 'velvet' dies off, and is removed by the stag rubbing his antlers against small trees and tree stumps, which become marked with scrapes and scars. Antler-rubbing goes on until the end of the rutting season, when the antlers eventually fall off. This behaviour may be important to the owner in familiarising himself with the shape and size of his antlers and thereby assessing his own physical prowess. During the rut, stags violently thrash the vegetation with their antlers, denuding and shredding the foliage.

Fallen antlers are easy to recognize by their shape and size, but not all antlers found in the forest are complete. Rats, mice and porcupines gnaw at them, and even deer eat some of them, presumably for calcium and other minerals. The question of why male deer annually cast their antlers and grow new ones — an apparently wasteful process which takes up a good deal of energy — is keenly debated by specialists, who have reached no definite conclusion. Some claim that in males it is a means of shedding excessive calcium; females use it up in making babies.

Actual remains of a kill are occasionally found. Small prey are quickly consumed, and little remains in the form of evidence. But large kills, such as those of the tiger, last longer and often reveal interesting facts or clues about the predator. If the kill is fresh the tracks round it may betray the identities of the killer or a scavenger, since most carnivores are quite opportunistic and will appropriate kill from others if they can. Tigers and leopards usually drag their kill into thick cover to avoid detection and lie up near it, if it is a large animal. Sometimes they also hide it by covering it with vegetation and debris, while the leopard may haul its kill up a tree. A tiger's kill can be distinguished from a leopard's by examining the bite marks on the neck; the holes made by tigers' teeth are larger and deeper, and the gap between the canines is wider. Tigers usually start feeding from the rump upwards and leopards from the belly.

Kills abandoned by the big cats are readily scavenged by smaller cats, carnivores and vultures, and wild boar may consume and scatter the remaining carcass. By counting the molars in the jaw of a kill, and examining the wear on them, experts can get some idea about the age and class of prey taken by predators.

Much can be learnt about an animal's feeding habits and diet from a study of its droppings. The shape, size, colour, texture and contents of scats all help narrow down the possibilities, but identifying scats is often more problematical than recognizing tracks. The characteristics of droppings change seasonally, since herbivores feeding on succulent vegetation produce soft and shapeless scats, quite different from the hard pellets which result from drier, coarser food.

Deer pellets vary from cylindrical to spherical. Size corresponds with the animal's body size, but there is considerable overlap. Gaur droppings are very similar to those of domestic cattle, though bulkier. Elephant dung, besides being in larger boluses, has a coarser texture than rhino dung, which is more compact and darker in colour. Rhinos frequently defecate in preferred latrine sites, where large quantities of dung accumulate over the years. This habit of resorting to a communal site is potentially dangerous, for if poachers discover the place, they sometimes dig a pit, which they then roof over with grass and branches, and trap the rhino when he comes about his daily business, or else ambush him with primitive firearms. The droppings of the omnivorous wild boar are dark, longish masses. The bulk of sloth bear droppings consist of insect and termite exoskeletons through most of the year, except in summer when they contain mainly fruit seeds.

Since herbivores eat large quantities of food, their droppings are commonly found, but since carnivores eat less and are also far less numerous, their scats are not easily found. They are usually cylindrical in shape and most difficult to tell apart. The tiger and the leopard defecate on scrape-marks made by their feet, and their scats may be distinguished from the size of the scrapes. Tough material such as hair, scales and fragments of bone passes out unaffected from a carnivore's digestive system, and an examination of these remains will usually determine what animal has been eaten. For instance, otter droppings consist largely of fish scales and bones. The hyena, on the other hand, has such powerful digestive juices that every bone is dissolved, and the bulk of its droppings sometimes consist of a paste of lime.

Many animals are themselves expert trackers, but with a difference: they read the signs with their noses, a skill which man has almost lost. Scent conveys far more information to mammals than we are inclined to think, and plays a vital role in their lives. Their specialised scent glands produce chemicals that are not only peculiar to their species but also differ from individual to individual. A tiger moving along a trail can thus tell not merely that *some* other tiger has also passed that way, but which one.

Mammals deposit and diffuse their smell in the environment in several ways. Glands between the toes transfer scent to the ground as they move. Scent is also usually imparted to droppings and urine, both of which furnish tigers, leopards, otters and other animals with strong olfactory signals.

Tigers have favourite trees on which they leave messages. They spray profusely along their territorial boundaries, both to inform other tigers that they are occupying the area, and, in the case of females, to give notice of their breeding condition. A tiger's scent mark on a tree can be recognized as a moist patch on the bark about 3 feet from the ground, although males spray higher than females. The squirt of a male makes a small patch, whereas the spray of a female spreads over a larger area.

Man cannot detect most mammal smells, but tigers and some other animals produce powerful stuff. When fresh, a tiger's spray can be smelt from some 15 feet away, but when exposed to the elements it decomposes quickly. Recently a sloth bear was seen rubbing itself against a tree, and this could well be a form of scent-marking, albeit perhaps one of only secondary importance.

Scent is also used by some animals as an effective means of defence. The anal glands of civets and some mongoose secrete such foul-smelling liquid that they effectively protect their owners from predators: enemies leave them alone and go hungry, rather than suffer the inconvenience of being smothered in their stink!

Yet another way of identifying unseen animals is by recognizing their calls. Except in the mating season most species generally remain quiet, but many have alarm-calls with which to signal danger. These calls, though difficult to render phonetically, are very distinctive, and give much information about what is going on in the jungle. The loud, abrupt *dhank!* of a startled sambar, for instance, is unmistakeable. If langurs persist with their hoarse alarm coughs — *kha-ko-kha, kha-ko-kha* — and are answered by the piping whistle of chital, one can be sure that a leopard or tiger has been spotted. Often the peacocks join in the chorus with their metallic honks until the whole jungle resounds with warnings. No one who has heard the deep, booming roar of a tiger will ever forget that sound; equally memorable is the 'sawing' of a leopard — the series of rasping grunts, on the in-breath and the out-breath, that sounds like someone cutting wood with a hand-saw.

15 Tourism

The history of tourism in the area is relatively short. The first lodge at Tiger Tops was built in the early 1960s — a small, four-bedroomed structure on stilts, rather in the style of Treetops Hotel in Kenya, with a large, circular building as a central restaurant and meeting place. The site was then on the south bank of the Rapti, just west of its confluence with the Reu, but later the Rapti changed course, carving itself a new channel directly westwards through the plains towards the Narayani, and leaving Tiger Tops on the bank of the smaller Reu.

The lodge, which proved a popular tourist attraction, was later extended to sleep forty visitors, but the man who originally ran it, John Coapman, found himself losing money. It was therefore taken over by Jim Edwards, at the time an executive with Pan American Airways, and Charles (Chuck) McDougal, an expert on tigers. Since then the lodge and the park have gone from strength to strength. Chitwan is now firmly on the map as a wildlife park of the highest international interest, and Tiger Tops has established itself as one of the most original and comfortable jungle lodges in the world.

Rather than concentrate a large number of tourists in one place, accommodation has been extended — and the load spread — by the construction of two satellite outposts. The first, a tented camp with twelve spacious safari tents whose location is changed every few years, was opened in 1974 some distance from Tiger Tops. The second, a Tharu longhouse with eight double rooms, was built outside the park boundary in 1980 to introduce visitors to the life and culture of the indigenous Tharu people. Meanwhile, by the mid-1970s, two independent establishments — Gaida Wildlife Camp and Hotel Elephant Camp — had sprung up at Sauraha, some 25 miles east of Tiger Tops, and other smaller camps and huts have recently mushroomed in the same area. All these cater for budget-conscious travellers, but because of their inadequate facilities they provide only limited opportunities of exploring the park. Tiger Tops and Gaida Wildlife Camp are park concessions and lie within its boundaries; the others operate from outside.

Between 1974 and 1981 the number of tourists arriving annually in Chitwan increased tenfold, from 836 to 8,464, the bulk of them coming to Tiger Tops. Yet the number of visitors has been deliberately kept down. Even when all three of Tiger Tops' locations are full, the total number of tourists in residence is only about seventy. Every precaution has been taken to minimise disruption of the environment and to strike a balance between tourism and conservation.

In spite of its richness in flora and fauna, and for all its scenic splendour, Chitwan has its limitations. By international standards the park is relatively small (although quite large by South Asian standards) and much of its hilly southern region is inaccessible to the ordinary traveller. The hills are also poor country for wildlife viewing, since it is very hard to see *anything* in their steep, forested ravines. Thus the park's capacity for carrying tourists is not very high, and it may well be that the present annual number of 8,000 (assuming that each person stays an average of three nights) is the practical ceiling. Above that, the environment would start to suffer. The jungle would lose its pristine freshness — until now carefully preserved — and it would become impossible to see animals in their natural setting without disturbing their routine. To aim any higher would probably be self-defeating, for tourists would not find what they had come to see.

At Tiger Tops itself a team of expert naturalists and *shikaris* is available to demonstrate every facet of jungle life: tiger-tracking, bird-watching, photography and butterfly-study are only a few of the activities on offer. Game-viewing can be done from elephant-back, by Land Rover, by boat or on foot.

What Tiger Tops has demonstrated is that it is perfectly possible to run a high-class tourist operation on a limited scale, and to make money without in any way damaging the environment. Indeed, far from doing harm, tourism has proved a positive benefit to the area, in that the various camps bring in much-needed revenue — over NER 800,000 in 1981 — and also give work to four hundred local people who otherwise would have no jobs.

This does not mean that the park has won universal approval in

Chitwan. Far from it. Most Nepalese, it must be admitted, are poor conservationists, and they have little interest in wildlife. At first it was incomprehensible to them that foreigners should come from all over the world, and pay enormous amounts of money, to see animals which they themselves take for granted. It is very hard to put over the need for wildlife conservation to people who are on a survival régime, and far more worried by the problem of where their next meal will come from than they are by the future of the tiger. To them the animals are a menace rather than an asset. How can you sell conservation to villagers living outside the park boundary when they know that every night the rhino come out to eat and trample their crops, that the deer, wild boar and birds do the same, and that every now and then a tiger or leopard will carry off one of their precious sheep, goats or buffalo?

The only way of putting over the message is by slow and patient education — by explaining not only that the park provides four hundred well-paid jobs, but that its very existence is vital to the people of the area. If it were swept away, and the forest were destroyed to make more farm land, the last remaining source of thatch grass and reeds (essential for house-building) would also disappear. The park authorities have recently instigated a system of discussions with local leaders and teachers. Meeting each year, they discuss the problems of the park and those of the villagers. Although grazing and uncontrolled collection of fuel wood cannot be permitted inside the park, the annual concession granted to the villagers for harvesting thatch grass is vital to their economy, and they have begun to realise that without the park they would be worse off, rather than better.

Ignorant though most Nepalese are of wildlife, the men who work in the wildlife wing at Tiger Tops (and the park as a whole) have strong superstitions about the forest, and consider it essential to propitiate the deities who dwell in the jungle. Twice a year, in summer and winter, our *shikaris* go out into the forest, select a suitable spot, and perform a *puja*, or traditional sacrifice and prayer.

The entire staff at Tiger Tops joins in the ceremony, in which goats and chicken are offered in sacrifice to the gods, goddesses and jungle spirits. After the head and blood have been offered, and prayers recited, the meat is cooked and everyone present joins in a pleasant party, with drinks and good food, which may last all day. An outsider might think the occasion light-hearted, but in fact it has the serious purpose of protecting those who work at Tiger Tops against wild animals. The fact that no accident with a wild animal has so far occurred is ascribed by everyone concerned to the correctness of the prayers and sacrifices offered to the jungle deities.

16   Chitwan today

Chitwan is a dynamic system, complete with its array of predators and prey and the habitat that supports them. It is regarded as one of the best-preserved national parks in Asia, not least because of the personal interest and support of our conservation-conscious Royal Family. The great aesthetic quality of the park has given rise to a viable tourist industry. But Chitwan is not without its difficulties — and in fact its problems are much the same as those that face the whole of Nepal, the Indian subcontinent, and most parts of third-world Asia. Chitwan may be taken as a classic example of the struggle between wildlife and man.

Because of its strange shape, the park has a very long boundary; despite the vigilance of the army inside, and the rhino patrol outside, protection is still a problem. Although no case of poaching has been reported inside the boundary since 1976, poaching for the pot, especially of deer and pigs, continues outside on a small scale.

This, however, is of little importance compared with the mass human assault on the very fabric of the jungle. On almost all sides the park is bounded by villages, and over the years the forest lines have steadily receded in the face of population growth. No one denies that the needs of the common man are basic and genuine: land for cultivation and housing, wood for fuel and building, fodder and graze for domestic stock. But with the human population of Chitwan growing annually at the rate of 3 per cent, the demands on the remaining forest resources are severe and increasing daily.

As one flies over the valley one sees mile after mile of cultivation in a mosaic of geometrical shapes north of the Rapti river. The park that lies south of the Rapti is still intact — thanks partly to the uncultivable, gravelly nature of the Siwalik Hills that has traditionally discouraged settlement — and indeed the endless terracing so common on the Mahabharat range is not found here. But in many areas of Chitwan no forest remains outside the park.

Domestic livestock have literally reduced all grazing to stubble, and whole tracts of forests have been eaten out of existence. Chitwan has one of the highest densities of domestic stock anywhere in the subcontinent: thousands of emaciated cattle and buffalo graze at the park's edge, and it is a major problem for the warden and the army guards to keep them out.

Nowhere is the contrast between protected and unprotected areas more starkly visible than on the airfield at Meghauli. There, a huge flat area of common land has been grazed down to a sward as smooth as a billiard-table. Yet immediately across the Rapti, as soon as one sets foot in the park, the grass is 20 feet high.

So acute is the shortage of fuel for cooking that villagers commonly use dried cow and buffalo dung cakes as a substitute for firewood. To supplement their requirements, hundreds of people illegally venture into the park to collect cattle fodder, building materials, bamboo, firewood, plant foods and other forest produce. Meanwhile, more and more ground is lost to housing: every new family means a new house on a new plot, thus cutting down still further the already meagre area of cultivable land.

With the construction of roads linking Chitwan to other parts of the country, the influx of people from northern Nepal and other areas has continued unabated. By 1971 the population had already reached 185,000. The clearing of new areas for agriculture continued throughout the 1970s. By 1981 the population had gone up to 250,000, and at the present rate of increase the figure will double by the year 2,000.

The original Tharus have become a minority, overwhelmed by the invasion of people from elsewhere.

It is the sheer numbers of humans that baffle the most vigorous conservation effort. Outside the park, man has far exceeded the threshhold of Chitwan's carrying capacity. But he does not understand the logic of conservation and does not plan long-term strategies; for him life is a question of survival, from day to day. The rhino and the deer that destroy his crops, and the tiger and the leopard that kill his domestic animals, can hardly be regarded as an asset from his point of view. Why these 'destructive' animals need to be conserved, he cannot see. From the other side of the Rapti all that the farmer sees is a large block of forest that can give him sustenance. He hardly realises that to destroy the forest would ultimately lead to his own destruction. But his annoyance is understandable, for restrictions recently imposed on him are unprecedented in their nature and consequences. Always, in the past, he and his ancestors have had a traditional right to forage in the forest. Why should they not do so now?

Illiterate as he is, he cannot grasp the need for conservation on a big scale. Nor can he understand the need for family-planning — and this brings us to the crux of the whole matter: how to combat human numbers?

According to one estimate, the annual consumption of wood in Nepal is one cubic metre per head. This means that Chitwan must have lost 250,000 cubic metres of wood in 1981 alone. From where will this loss be replaced, if forests are shrinking all the time? How will the forest be able to produce 500,000 cubic metres of wood in the year 2005? Nature is highly resilient, but with this kind of slaughter, it simply gives in.

Chitwan is not an island, and so cannot be treated in isolation. Its fate is closely linked with that of the country in the north. The situation in the hills, far from being better, is even worse — and the ecological disasters occurring there send repercussions far down into the plains. Once the forest cover is removed from the mountains, the ground loses its capacity to retain water, and the topsoil is quickly eroded by the combined action of wind and water. (It is said that the fertile topsoil which gets washed away in every monsoon flood is Nepal's major export.) In the mountains the process deals death to an agriculture-based economy: the land becomes sick, and productivity declines. In the plains the effect is equally damaging: heavy siltation fills up the river beds and forces them to expand horizontally when they flood, causing widespread habitat-destruction. In the rivers themselves deep-water creatures such as dolphins suffer from the degradation of their environment.

It is essential that the Siwalik range is left untouched, to conserve the watershed areas which are especially fragile. Because of the loose soil and the sloping ground, any disturbance of the present pattern would cause instant erosion in the hills and habitat-degradation downstream.

The narrow belt of floodplain, on the other hand, needs positive management. The pattern of vegetation there has changed considerably in the past ten years — the wetlands are drying up, tall grasses predominate where short grasses once stood, and the forests are gradually spreading. These are natural processes, but they have created conditions unfavourable for wildlife by lowering the area's carrying capacity.

Protection alone is not going to maintain the integrity of the floodplain: scientific management is needed. The vegetation may have to be manipulated so as to create open patches in the tall grassland and forest. The wetlands will have to be restored, for example by the eradication of water hyacinth, which is prematurely killing the lakes.

The clearing of patches will favour short grass such as *Imperata*, and this in turn will support larger numbers of animals, provide better wildlife sighting facilities for tourists and ensure a steady supply of thatch grass for the villagers. (Without positive management this commodity will be depleted in years to come.)

Nor are Chitwan's problems only ecological: they are socio-economic as well. The conflict, or rather competition, between man and wildlife can be resolved only by allowing the local people some form of direct benefit from the park. Already it provides them with thatching material and reeds for house-building, and this concession should be continued, to ensure their support. Efforts must be made to explore further ways of reconciling the needs of the park and the people to ensure Chitwan's future.

Other problems abound. Overfishing in the rivers, streams and lakes, which has depleted the stocks of fish, is reflected in the dwindling populations of fishing raptors and other water birds. Nor do development and conservation go together. The barrage across the Narayani at Tribenighat, on the India-Nepal border, was built to further irrigation schemes, but it lacks an adequate fish-ladder, so that fish cannot easily pass the dam on their way upstream. Gharials and dolphins, once past the barrage, can never return upriver. If chemical wastes from the proposed paper-pulp factory at Gaidakot, near Narayangar, are released into the Narayani, they are bound to damage the aquatic life of the river.

The proposed extension of the national park to 500 square miles will go a long way towards maintaining the ecological integrity of the region. The fact that, in spite of all its poverty, such a large area can still be secured for wildlife is a fine example of national commitment to the cause of conservation. Yet far too many people remain oblivious to the threat of overpopulation. Without controlling human numbers, one cannot hope to save the habitat that supports wildlife. Ironically it is humans, rather than animals, that urgently need to be managed before it is too late.

The day of reckoning can be put off by monumental efforts at rehabilitation. A nationwide scheme of reafforestation must be launched, perhaps on the lines suggested by the Indian expert Shankar Ranganathan, who produced plans for an immense agro-forestry industry which he hoped would provide farmers with despereately-needed fodder and fuel. His idea was inspired by two concurrent facts: one, that India (like Nepal) is overpopulated and losing forests at a terrifying rate, and two, that the subcontinent has millions unemployed. Put the people to work planting trees, and you would soon have new forests, which could be cropped scientifically on a sustained-yield basis.

Some such scheme, I believe, must be started in Nepal. What we need is a grass-roots movement in which the *panchayat*, or village administration, will be entrusted with the task of growing trees — preferably indigenous types, but fast-growing species — so that each area has enough artificial, cultivated woodland to supply its people regularly with fuel and fodder, without destroying any more of the natural forest.

Purists argue that it is unwise to start monocultures, because a couple of fast-growing species could in theory ruin an area's ecology. They have a point. But in my view the situation is now so grave that we simply must take the pressure off whatever forest we have left: there is no time to argue about monocultures, or the last remnant will be gone.

Without some radical initiative of this kind, it is most unlikely that the remaining forests outside the park will meet the requirements of the people much longer. The farmers will be forced to make increasing inroads into the park out of sheer instinct for survival. At the moment 58,000 square miles of forests are being destroyed every year — which means that a forest area the size of the Chitwan park is being lost every 2.3 days! The wildlife — the very existence — of Chitwan is in great danger, and to save it is not merely a national but a global responsibility. If Chitwan goes, yet one more paradise will be lost for ever.

APPENDIX A

Birds of Chitwan

Ratings
1 = rare
2 = less rare
3 = occasional
4 = fairly common
5 = common
6 = very common

PODICIPEDIDAE
1 Great Crested Grebe
(Podiceps cristatus) 1; on lakes;
winter visitor, October — April.
2 Little Grebe *(Podiceps
ruficollis)* 1-2; on lakes and on
the Narayani; winter visitor
and/or passage migrant.

PHALACROCORACIDAE
3 Large Cormorant
(Phalacrocorax carbo) 5; on the
Narayani and the Rapti; winter
visitor, October — April; fishing
flocks of several hundred
occasionally seen; attain full
breeding plumage by March.
4 Little Cormorant
(Phalacrocorax niger) 2; on
lakes; irregular winter visitor,
October — April.
5 Darter *(Anhinga rufa)* 5; on
swamps, lakes and occasionally
near rivers; resident; confirmed
breeding.

ARDEIDAE
6 Grey Heron *(Ardea cinerea)* 4;
on marshes and large rivers;
winter visitor, August — April,
resident minority; possible
breeding.
7 Purple Heron *(Ardea

purpurea) 4; on swamps and
lakes; mainly winter visitor,
October — April; some resident,
possible breeding.
8 Little Green Heron *(Butorides
striatus)* 4; along rivers and
lakes; resident; numbers
augmented in summer;
confirmed breeding.
9 Pond Heron *(Ardeola grayii)*
6; on marshes, edges of lakes
and along rivers; resident;
confirmed breeding.
10 Night Heron *(Nycticorax
nycticorax)* 5; on edges of lakes;
resident; confirmed breeding.
11 Cattle Egret *(Bubulcus ibis)*
4; along the park boundaries
near cattle; resident; confirmed
breeding (outside the park).
12 Large Egret *(Egretta alba)* 4;
along rivers, lakes and marshes;
resident; confirmed breeding.
13 Intermediate Egret *(Egretta
intermedia)* 4; along rivers and
marshes; resident; confirmed
breeding.
14 Little Egret *(Egretta
garzetta)* 5; along rivers and
marshes; resident; confirmed
breeding.
15 Chestnut Bittern *(Ixobrychus
cinnamomeus)* 3; in grassland
swamps; resident; numbers
increase in summer; confirmed
breeding.
16 Yellow Bittern *(Ixobrychus
sinensis)* 2; in grassland
marshes; summer visitor May
— October; confirmed breeding.
17 Black Bittern *(Dupetor

flavicollis) 1; sight record by T.
& C. Inskipp, April 1980; edges
of lakes; vagrant.

CICONIIDAE
18 Painted Stork *(Ibis
leucocephalus)* 1-2; on the
banks of the Narayani; summer
visitor May — October.
19 Openbill Stork *(Anastomus
oscitans)* 5; on grassland,
marshes and near lakes;
resident; confirmed breeding.
20 Whitenecked Stork *(Ciconia
episcopus)* 3; on grassland,
marshes and near lakes and
rivers; resident; confirmed
breeding.
21 White Stork *(Ciconia
ciconia)* 1; near lakes and rivers;
winter visitor October — May;
passage migrant.
22 Black Stork *(Ciconia nigra)*
4; along open river banks;
winter visitor October — April.
23 Blacknecked Stork
(Xenorhynchus asiaticus) 2;
along open river beds; winter
visitor October — April.
24 Lesser Adjutant Stork
(Leptoptilos javanicus) 3; on
grassland swamps, near open
river beds; resident; confirmed
breeding.

GRUIDAE
25 Common Crane *(Grus grus)*
4; along sandy banks of the
Narayani; winter visitor October
— March; large numbers overfly
on migration

October/November and March/April.

26 Sarus Crane *(Grus antigone)*; only a few sight records at the edge of the park; in wet fields and cultivation; vagrant.

27 Demoiselle Crane *(Anthropoides virgo)* 4; along the Narayani; passage migrant in October/November and April/May; some winter visitors.

THRESKIORNITHIDAE

28 Black Ibis *(Pseudibis papillosa)* 5; along sandy river banks; resident; confirmed breeding.

ANATIDAE

29 Greylag Goose *(Anser anser)* 1; on the Narayani; winter visitor October — April.

30 Barheaded Goose *(Anser indicus)* 2; on the Narayani; winter visitor October — April.

31 Whistling Swan *(Cygnus columbianus)* 1; first sighted in Nepal on 23 February 1978 on the Narayani. Subsequently seen several times in March of that year; vagrant.

32 Lesser Whistling Teal *(Dendrocygna javanica)* 5; on lakes and swamps and occasionally on rivers; resident; confirmed breeding.

33 Ruddy Sheldrake *(Tadorna ferruginea)* 6; on rivers; winter visitor September/October — April/May.

34 Pintail *(Anas acuta)* 3; along the Narayani and lakes; winter visitor October — April; large flocks may be seen in February/March.

35 Common Teal *(Anas crecca)* 4; on lakes and sluggish channels of rivers; winter visitor September — April.

36 Garganey *(Anas querquedula)* 1; on rivers and

the sluggish channels of the Narayani; passage migrant August/September and March/April.

37 Spotbill Duck *(Anas peocilorhyncha)* 1-2; on lakes, ponds and sluggish channels of the Narayani; irregular winter visitor.

38 Mallard *(Anas platyrhynchos)* 2; on rivers; winter visitor October — March.

39 Gadwall *(Anas strepera)* 2; on ponds and sluggish channels of the Narayani; winter visitor October — March/April.

40 Falcated Teal *(Anas falcata)* 1; only a few sight records; on ponds and sluggish waters; winter visitor October — April.

41 Wigeon *(Anas penelope)* 2; on ponds and sluggish channels of the Narayani; passage migrant; large flocks seen in March/April.

42 Shoveler *(Anas clypeata)* 2; on ponds and slow channels of rivers; winter visitor or passage migrants November and April/May.

43 Redcrested Pochard *(Netta rufina)* 2; on rivers; winter visitor November — April; numbers increase in spring.

44 Common Pochard *(Aythya ferina)* 2; on rivers and ponds; winter visitor November — March/April; numbers increase in March.

45 White-eyed Pochard *(Aythya nyroca)* 1; sight record on the Narayani in November 1980; passage migrant.

46 Tufted Duck *(Aythya fuligula)* 2; on ponds and slow waters of the Narayani; passage migrant March/April (43 cm).

47 Cotton Teal *(Nettapus coromandelianus)* 2; on lakes; winter visitor November — April/May.

48 Goldeneye Duck *(Bucephala clangula)* 1; on lakes and rivers; winter visitor October — April; a few sight records.

49 Smew *(Mergus albellus)* 1; sight record on the Narayani in February 1983; vagrant.

50 Merganser *(Margus merganser)* 5; on the Rapti and the Narayani; winter visitor October — April.

ACCIPITRIDAE

51 Black-crested Baza *(Aviceda leuphotes)* 1; in riverine forest; summer visitor March — June; confirmed breeding.

52 Black-shouldered Kite *(Elanus caeruleus)* 3; in riverine forest and open savanna; resident; possible breeding.

53 Crested Honey Kite *(Pernis ptilorhyncus)* 5; in sal and riverine forests; resident; possible breeding.

54 Dark Kite *(Milvus migrans)* 5; at edges of the park and near human settlements; winter visitor October — May.

55 Brahminy Kite *(Haliastur indus)* 1; over open country near the Rapti river; a few sight records in winter.

56 Goshawk *(Accipiter gentilis)* 1-2; over forests and grasslands and open country; winter visitor October — April.

57 Crested Goshawk *(Accipiter trivirgatus)* 2; in sal and riverine forests; winter visitor (possible resident).

58 Sparrow Hawk *(Accipiter nisus)* 1; recorded by Dr J. M. Thiollay in October/November; perhaps a winter visitor.

59 Besra Sparrow Hawk *(Accipiter virgatus)* 1; sal and riverine forests; winter visitor?

60 Shikra *(Accipiter badius)* 4; in sal and riverine forests; resident; confirmed breeding.

61 Long-legged Buteo *(Buteo*

rufinus) 1; recorded near water by Dr J. M. Thiollay in October/November 1978; winter visitor.

62 Eurasian Buteo *(Buteo buteo)* 1; in open country; winter visitor October — April/passage migrant.

63 White-eyed Hawk *(Butastur teesa)* 4; in riverine forest and open savanna; resident; confirmed breeding.

64 Crested Serpent Eagle *(Spilornis cheela)* 5; in sal and riverine forests; resident; confirmed breeding.

65 Mountain Hawk Eagle *(Spizaetus nipalensis)* 2; in sal and hill forests; winter visitor October — April.

66 Changeable Hawk Eagle *(Spizaetus limnaeetus)* 2; in sal and riverine forests; resident, confirmed breeding.

67 Rufous-bellied Hawk Eagle *(Lophotriorchis kienerii)* 1; in sal and riverine forests; resident?

68 Booted Eagle *(Hieraaetus pennatus)* 2; in sal and riverine forests; winter visitor.

69 Tawny Eagle *(Aquila rapax)* 2; in riverine and open forests and dry river beds; winter visitor October — April; possible breeding.

70 Steppe Eagle *(Aquila nipalensis)* 2; in riverine forest and open savanna; winter visitor October/November — March/April.

71 Greater Spotted Eagle *(Aquila clanga)* 1; in riverine forests and near water; winter visitor October — April.

72 Lesser Spotted Eagle *(Aquila pomarina)* 2; in riverine forest/savanna and open country; winter visitor October — March/April.

73 White-tailed Sea Eagle *(Haliaeetus albicilla)* 2; in

forests bordering rivers; winter visitor November — April.

74 Black Eagle *(Ictinaetus malayensis)* 1; in sal and hill forests and over grasslands; winter visitor, October — May; possible breeding.

75 Pallas's Fishing Eagle *(Haliaeetus leucoryphus)* 1; along forests bordering rivers, near lakes and marshes; winter visitor October — April; possible breeding.

76 Grey-headed Fishing Eagle *(Icthyophaga icthyaetus)* 2; in forests near lakes and swamps and streams; resident; confirmed breeding.

77 Himalayan Grey-headed Fishing Eagle *(Icthyophaga nana)* 1; in forests near lakes, swamps and streams; resident; confirmed breeding.

78 Black Vulture *(Torgos calvus)* 2; in sal forest and in open country; winter visitor September/October — April; possible breeding.

79 Cinereous Vulture *(Aegypius monachus)* 1; in sal forest and in open country; winter visitor November — March.

80 Eurasian Griffon *(Gyps fulvus)* 4; in sal and adjoining forests and in open country; winter visitor October — April.

81 Indian Griffon *(Gyps indicus)* 4; in sal and adjoining forests and in open country; resident?; confirmed breeding.

82 White-backed Vulture *(Gyps bengalensis)* 5; in sal and adjoining forests and in open country; resident?; confirmed breeding.

83 Egyptian Vulture *(Neophron percnopterus)* 3; in open country along the park boundaries; winter visitor October — May.

84 Hen Harrier *(Circus cyaneus)* 3; in riverine forest/savanna and over open

expanses of grassland and marshes; winter visitor September/October — April/May.

85 Pale Harrier *(Circus macrourus)* 1; in savanna, grassland and open country; winter visitor October — April.

86 Montagu's Harrier *(Circus pygargus)* 1; in grassland, open country and near water; passage migrant March/April.

87 Pied Harrier *(Circus melanoleucos)* 2; in savanna, grassland and open country near water; winter visitor October — April.

88 Marsh Harrier *(Circus aeruginosus)* 4; in grassland marshes, savanna and over open river beds; winter visitor October — April.

89 Osprey *(Pandion haliaetus)* 4; along rivers, streams, lakes and marshes; resident; numbers increase in winter; possible breeding; mating display.

FALCONIDAE

90 Red-thighed Falconet *(Microhierax caerulescens)* 1; in sal and riverine forests and savanna; resident?/passage migrant.

91 Laggar Falcon *(Falco jugger)* rare; in open country; resident?

92 Shaheen Falcon *(Falco peregrinus peregrinator)* 1; in sal and riverine forests; winter visitor October — April.

93 Oriental Hobby *(Falco severus)* 1; in sal and riverine forests; winter visitor October — April.

94 Eurasian Hobby *(Falco subbuteo)* 1; in open forests and savanna; winter visitor October — April.

95 Red-headed Merlin *(Falco chicquera)* 1; in riverine forest, savanna and open country; winter visitor?

96 Red-legged Falcon *(Falco vespertinus)* 1; in open country; passage migrant.
97 Lesser Kestrel *(Falco naumanni)* 1; in open country and savanna; passage migrant.
98 Eurasian Kestrel *(Falco tinnunculus)* 1-2; in savanna, grassland and in open country; winter visitor October — April.

PHASIANIDAE
99 Black Partridge *(Francolinus francolinus)* 4; in grassland; resident; possible breeding.
100 Grey Quail *(Coturnix coturnix)* 4; in grassland; resident?; possible breeding.
101 Blue-breasted Quail *(Coturnix chinensis)* 1; in sal forest/grassland; resident; possible breeding.
102 Kalij Pheasant *(Lophura leucomelana)* 3; associated with sal forest; resident; confirmed breeding.
103 Common Peafowl *(Pavo cristatus)* 5; in riverine forest/grassland and on river banks; resident; confirmed breeding.
104 Red Jungle Fowl *(Gallus gallus)* 5; in riverine forest/grassland and edge of sal forest; resident; confirmed breeding.

TURNICIDAE
105 Button Quail *(Turnix tanki)* 4; in grasslands; resident; possible breeding.
106 Little Bustard-Quail *(Turnix sylvatica)* 3; in grasslands; resident; possible breeding.
107 Common Bustard-Quail *(Turnix suscitator)* 5; in grasslands; resident; possible breeding.

RALLIDAE
108 Baillon's Crake *(Porzana*

pusilla) 1; in grassland swamps and reedy edges of lakes; winter visitor October — April.
109 Ruddy Crake *(Amaurornis fuscus)* 3-4; in grassland marshes and near lakes; resident; possible breeding.
110 Brown Crake *(Amaurornis akool)* 5; in grassland marshes and edges of lakes and streams; resident; confirmed breeding.
111 White-breasted Waterhen *(Amaurornis phoenicurus)* 5; in grassland marshes/wetlands and edges of lakes; resident; confirmed breeding.
112 Indian Gallinule *(Gallinula chloropus)* 6; on lakes and grassland swamps; winter visitor May — October; resident.
113 Purple Gallinule *(Porphyrio porphyrio)* 3; on lakes; winter visitor September/October — May.
114 Coot *(Fulica atra)* 1-2; on lakes; winter visitor October — April.

OTIDIDAE
115 Bengal Florican *(Eupodotis bengalensis)* 3; in short grasslands; resident/ summer visitor; possible breeding.

JACANIDAE
116 Pheasant-tailed Jacana *(Hydrophasianus chirurgus)* 1; on lakes with floating vegetation and in marshes; summer visitor March — October; possible breeding.
117 Bronze-winged Jacana *(Metopidius indicus)* 4; on lakes with floating vegetation and in marshes; resident; possible breeding.

CHARADRIIDAE
118 Red-wattled Lapwing *(Vanellus indicus)* 5; along river banks; resident; confirmed

breeding.
119 Spur-winged Lapwing *(Vanellus spinosus)* 5; along river banks; resident; confirmed breeding.
120 Eurasian Lapwing *(Vanellus vanellus)* 1; along river banks; winter visitor October — April.
121 Yellow-wattled Lapwing *Vanellus malabaricus)* 1; dry river beds and open areas at edge of park; winter visitor.
122 Eastern Golden Plover *(Pluvialis dominica)* 1-2; on wet mud banks along park's edge; passage migrant?; sight records in April. Several hundred seen at Meghauli late October/early November 1981.
123 Little Ringed Plover *(Charadrius dubius)* 5; on river banks and mudflats; resident (numbers increase in winter); confirmed breeding.
124 Kentish Plover *(Charadrius alexandrinus)* 3; along shingle and sand beds of rivers; winter visitor October — April.
125 Lesser Sand Plover *(Charadrius mongolus)* rare/vagrant; on river banks; winter visitor/passage migrant.
126 Whimbrel *(Numenius phaeopus)* rare; on mudflats and riverbanks; passage migrant April — September.
127 Curlew *(Numenius arquata)* 1; on mudflats and river banks; passage migrant; small flocks in September and again in April.
128 Common Redshank *(Tringa totanus)* 2; on river banks and mudflats; winter visitor September — April.
129 Spotted Redshank *(Tringa erythropus)* 1-2; along rivers and mudflats; winter visitor September — April.
130 Greenshank *(Tringa nebularia)* 6; along river banks;

winter visitor August/October
— April/May.
131 Marsh Sandpiper *(Tringa
stagnatilis)* 1; along mudbanks
of rivers; winter visitor
September — April.
132 Green Sandpiper *(Tringa
ochropus)* 5; along river and
stream and banks; winter visitor
September — April.
133 Wood Sandpiper *(Tringa
glareola)* 3; on river banks;
winter visitor September —
April.
134 Common Sandpiper
(Tringa hypoleucos) 5; on river
and stream banks; winter visitor
August/September — April.
135 Temminck's Stint *(Calidris
temminckii)* 5; on river and
stream banks; winter visitor
August/October — April.
136 Little Stint *(Calidris
minutus)* rare; vagrant?; on river
banks and stream banks; winter
visitor/passage migrant.
137 Pintail Snipe *(Capella
stenura)* 1; on stonebeds and
margins of shallow and sluggish
channels of rivers; winter visitor
September to April.
138 Fantail Snipe *(Capella
gallinago)* 3; in sluggish
channels of and along rivers;
winter visitor September —
April.

ROSTRATULIDAE
139 Painted Snipe *(Rostratula
benghalensis)* 2; along edges of
lakes and marshes; resident;
possible breeding.

RECURVIROSTRIDAE
140 Black-winged Stilt
(Himantopus himantopus) 1;
along rivers and marshes;
winter visitor October — April.

BURHINIDAE
141 Eurasian Thick Knee
(Burhinus oedicnemus) 4; along

river banks and dry sand/stone
beds; resident; confirmed
breeding.
142 Great Thick Knee *(Esacus
magnirostris)* 3; along river
banks and stone beds; resident;
confirmed breeding.

GLAREOLIDAE
143 Small Pratincole *(Glareola
lactea)* 6; along river banks;
resident; confirmed breeding.

LARIDAE
144 Herring Gull *(Larus
argentatus)* 1; sight records
along the Narayani; perhaps a
passage migrant.
145 Great Black-headed Gull
(Larus ichthyactus) 4; on rivers;
winter visitor October — April.
146 Black-headed Gull *(Larus
ribibundus)* 3; on rivers; winter
visitor September — April.
147 Brown-headed Gull *(Larus
brunnicephalus)* 1-2; on rivers;
winter visitor September —
March.
148 Caspian Tern
(Hydroprogne caspia) 1; on
rivers; winter visitor?/passage
migrant.
149 Indian River Tern *(Sterna
aurantia)* 4; on rivers; resident;
possible breeding.
150 Common Tern *(Sterna
hirundo)* 1; on rivers and lakes;
passage migrant.
151 Black-bellied Tern *(Sterna
acuticauda)* 5; on rivers and
lakes; resident; possible
breeding.
152 Little Tern *(Sterna
albifrons)* 4; on rivers; summer
visitor March to September;
possible breeding.

COLUMBIDAE
153 Pintail Green Pigeon
(Treron apicauda) 1; recorded in
the upper sal forest by
Dr J.M. Thiollay in

October/November 1978;
resident; possible breeding.
154 Thick-billed Green Pigeon
(Treron curvirostra) 1; in sal
and riverine forests; resident;
possible breeding.
155 Orange-breasted Green
Pigeon *(Treron bicincta)* 5; in
sal and riverine forests;
resident; confirmed breeding.
156 Grey-fronted Green Pigeon
(Treron pompadora) 5; in sal
and riverine forests; resident;
confirmed breeding.
157 Bengal Green Pigeon
(Treron phoenicoptera) 4; in sal
and riverine forests; resident;
possible breeding.
158 Imperial Pigeon *(Ducula
badia)* 1; recorded in riverine
forest by Dr J. M. Thiollay in
October/November 1978;
resident?; possible breeding.
159 Blue Rock Pigeon
(Columba livia) 4; on rocky
cliffs and banks of rivers and
forest streams; several hundred
roosting on the banks of the
Narayani near Kana khola in
February 1981; resident;
possible breeding.
160 Rufous Turtle Dove
(Streptopelia orientalis) 3; in sal
and riverine forests; winter
visitor October — April.
161 Red Turtle Dove
(Streptopelia tranquebarica) 3;
in sal and riverine forests;
resident; confirmed breeding.
162 Indian Ring Dove
(Streptopelia decaocto) 3; in sal
and riverine forests and
grasslands; resident; confirmed
breeding.
163 Spotted Dove *(Streptopelia
chinensis)* 6; in sal/riverine
forests and grasslands; resident;
confirmed breeding.
164 Emerald Dove
(Chalcophaps indica) 4; in sal
and damp riverine forests;
resident; confirmed breeding.

PSITTACIDAE
165 Rose-ringed Parakeet *(Psittacula krameri)* 6; in sal and riverine forests; resident; confirmed breeding.
166 Large Parakeet *(Psittacula eupatria)* 5; in sal and riverine forests; resident; confirmed breeding.
167 Rose-breasted Parakeet *(Psittacula alexandri)* 6; in sal and riverine forests; resident; confirmed breeding.
168 Blossom-headed Parakeet *(Psittacula cyanocephala)* 4; in sal and riverine forests; resident; confirmed breeding.
169 Slaty-headed Parakeet *(Psittacula himalayana)* 1; in sal and riverine forests; winter visitor? October — March.
170 Indian Lorikeet *(Loriculus vernalis)* 1; in sal and riverine forests; resident?; possible breeding.

CUCULIDAE
171 Pied Crested Cuckoo *(Clamator jacobinus)* 2; in sal and riverine forests; summer visitor May — October; possible breeding.
172 Red-winged Crested Cuckoo *(Clamator coromandus)* 3; in sal and riverine forests; summer visitor April — October; confirmed breeding.
173 Large Hawk Cuckoo *(Caculus sparverioides)* 1; in riverine forests; recorded by T. & C. Inskipp in April 1980; passage migrant.
174 Common Hawk Cuckoo *(Cuculus varius)* 5; in riverine forests; summer visitor January to October or resident?; possible breeding.
175 Eurasian Cuckoo *(Cuculus canorus)* 3; in sal and riverine forests; summer visitor March — September; possible breeding.

176 Indian Cuckoo *(Cuculus micropterus)* 4; in sal and riverine forests; summer visitor February — September; confirmed breeding.
177 Banded Bay Cuckoo *(Cacomantis sonneratii)* 2; in sal and riverine forests; summer visitor February — October; possible breeding.
178 Plaintive Cuckoo *(Cacomantis merulinus)* 2; in sal and riverine forests; summer visitor April — October; possible breeding.
179 Emerald Cuckoo *(Chalcites maculatus)* 1; in riverine forests; passage migrant.
180 Drongo Cuckoo *(Surniculus lugubris)* 5; in sal and riverine forests, summer visitor April — October; confirmed breeding.
181 Large Green-billed Malkoha *(Rhopodytes tristis)* 3; in sal and riverine forests; resident; confirmed breeding.
182 Koel Cuckoo *(Eudynamys scolopacea)* 2; in sal and riverine forests; summer visitor March — September; possible breeding.
183 Sirkeer Cuckoo *(Taccocua leschenaultii)* 1; in sal and riverine forests; resident?; possible breeding.
184 Small Coucal *(Centropus toulou)* 4; in grasslands; resident; numbers increase in summer; confirmed breeding.
185 Large Coucal *(Centropus sinensis)* 5; in grasslands; resident; confirmed breeding.

STRIGIDAE
186 Grass Owl *(Tyto capensis)* 2; in tall grassland; resident; confirmed breeding.
187 Scops Owl *(Otus scops)* 5; in sal and riverine forests; resident; confirmed breeding.
188 Collared Scops Owl *(Otus bakkamoena)* 2; in sal and

riverine forests; resident; confirmed breeding.
189 Forest Eagle Owl *(Bubo nipalensis)* 2; in sal and dense riverine forests; resident; confirmed breeding.
190 Tawny Fish Owl *(Bubo flavipes)* 1; recorded in the upper sal forest by Dr J.M.Thiollay in October/November 1978; resident; possible breeding.
191 Brown Fish Owl *(Bubo zeylonensis)* 2; near water in sal and riverine forests, resident; possible breeding.
192 Barred Owlet *(Glaucidium cuculoides)* 4; in sal and riverine forests; resident; confirmed breeding.
193 Jungle Owlet *(Glaucidium radiatum)* 5; in sal and riverine forests; resident; confirmed breeding.
194 Spotted Owlet *(Athene brama)* 2; in sal/riverine forests and savannah; resident; confirmed breeding.
195 Brown Hawk Owl *(Ninox scutulata)* 4; in sal and riverine forests; resident; confirmed breeding.
196 Short-eared Owl *(Assio flammeus)* 1; recorded by Dr J.M.Thiollay in October/November 1978; perhaps a winter visitor.

CAPRIMULGIDAE
197 Long-tailed Nightjar *(Caprimulgus macrurus)* 4; in sal/riverine forests and grasslands; summer visitor?; February/March — October/November; confirmed breeding.
198 Jungle Nightjar *(Caprimulgus indicus)* 4; in sal forests and adjoining areas; passage migrant?
199 Little Nightjar *(Caprimulgus asiaticus)* 1; in

open forests; heard in spring; summer visitor?; possible breeding.
200 Franklin's Nightjar *(Caprimulgus affinis)* 4; along river beds and adjoining forest/grasslands; summer visitor March — August; confirmed breeding.

TROGONIDAE
201 Red-headed Trogon *(Harpactes erythrocephalus)* 2; in sal forests, especially in bamboo stands; possible breeding.

CORACIIDAE
202 Dark Roller *(Eurystomus orientalis)* 5; in sal and riverine forests; summer visitor April — September/October; confirmed breeding.
203 Indian Roller *(Coracias benghalensis)* 5; in riverine and sal forests; resident; confirmed breeding.

UPUPIDAE
204 Hoopoe *(Upupa epops)* 4; in riverine forests and grasslands; resident?; (absent during monsoons); confirmed breeding.

ALCEDINIDAE
205 Small Pied Kingfisher *(Ceryle rudis)* 5; on rivers; resident; confirmed breeding.
206 Large Pied Kingfisher *(Ceryle lugubris)* 1; along forest rivers; resident?; vagrant.
207 Eurasian Kingfisher *(Alcedo atthis)* 4; along rivers and lakes; resident; confirmed breeding.
208 Blue-eared Kingfisher *(Alcedo meninting)* 2; in sal forest streams and occasionally near lakes; resident; possible breeding.
209 Stork-billed Kingfisher

(Pelargopsis capensis) 3; along rivers and near lakes; resident; confirmed breeding.
210 White-breasted Kingfisher *(Halcyon smyrnensis)* 5; along rivers and lakes; resident; confirmed breeding.
211 Black-capped Kingfisher *(Halcyon pileata)* 1; along rivers; vagrant.

MEROPIDAE
212 Chestnut-headed Bee-eater *(Merops leschenaulti)* 6; in riverine forest/grassland and along edges of sal forests; summer visitor? February — October; minority resident; confirmed breeding.
213 Blue-tailed Bee-eater *(Merops philippinus)* 4; along lakes and streams in riverine forest/grasslands; summer visitor March — September; possible breeding.
214 Green Bee-eater *(Merops orientalis)* 5; in riverine forest/grasslands; summer visitor February — October or resident?; confirmed breeding.
215 Blue-bearded Bee-eater *(Nyctyornis athertoni)* 2; in riverine forest/grasslands and along the edges of sal forests; resident; possible breeding.

BUCEROTIDAE
216 Grey Hornbill *(Tockus birostris)* 1; in sal and riverine forests; resident?; possible breeding.
217 Pied Hornbill *(Anthracoceros malabaricus)* 4; in sal and riverine forests; resident; confirmed breeding.
218 Giant Hornbill *(Buceros bicornis)* 3; in sal and riverine forests; resident; confirmed breeding.

CAPITONIDAE
219 Lineated Barbet

(Megalaima lineata) 5; in sal and riverine forests; resident; confirmed breeding.
220 Blue-throated Barbet *(Megalaima asiatica)* 3; in sal and riverine forests; resident; confirmed breeding.
221 Crimson-breasted Barbet *(Megalaima haemacephala)* 2; in sal forest and occasionally in riverine forest; resident?; possible breeding.

PICIDAE
222 Wryneck *(Jynx torquilla)* 2; in riverine forest/ grasslands; winter visitor October — April/passage migrant.
223 Rufous Piculet *(Sasia ochracea)* 1; in sal forests; resident; possible breeding.
224 Spotted Piculet *(Picumnus innominatus)* 1; in sal forest; resident; possible breeding.
225 Grey-crowned Pigmy Woodpecker *(Dendrocopos canicapillus)* 5; in riverine and sal forests; resident; confirmed breeding.
226 Brown-crowned Pigmy Woodpecker *(Dendrocopos nanus)* 1; in riverine forests; vagrant.
227 Small Scaly-bellied Woodpecker *(Picus xanthopygaeus)* 4; in riverine and sal forests; resident; possible breeding.
228 Black-naped Woodpecker *(Picus canus)* 4; in sal and riverine forests; resident; confirmed breeding.
229 Large Yellow-naped Woodpecker *(Picus flavinucha)* 3; in sal and riverine forests; resident; possible breeding.
230 Small Yellow-naped Woodpecker *(Picus chlorolophus)* 4; in sal and riverine forests; resident; possible breeding.
231 Lesser Golden-backed

Woodpecker *(Dinopium benghalense)* 3; in monotypic sal and open forests; resident; possible breeding.
232 Three-toed Golden-backed Woodpecker *(Dinopium shorii)* 5; in sal and riverine forests; resident; confirmed breeding.
233 Large Golden-backed Woodpecker *(Chrysocolaptes lucidus)* 4; in sal and riverine forests; resident; confirmed breeding.
234 Fulvous-breasted Pied Woodpecker *(Dendrocopos macei)* 4; in sal and riverine forests; resident; confirmed breeding.
235 Yellow-fronted Pied Woodpecker *(Dendrocopos mahrattensis)* 1; in riverine forests; resident?; confirmed breeding.
236 Brown Woodpecker *(Micropterus brachyurus)* 2; in sal and riverine forests; resident; confirmed breeding.
237 Great Slaty Woodpecker *(Mulleripicus pulverulentus)* 1; in deep sal forest; resident; possible breeding.

EURYLAIMIDAE
238 Long-tailed Broadbill *(Psarisomus dalhousiae)* 1; in sal forests near streams; resident?; possible breeding.

PITTIDAE
239 Indian Pitta *(Pitta brachyura* 5; in sal and thick riverine forests; summer visitor April — October; confirmed breeding.
240 Green-breasted Pitta *(Pitta sordida)* 5; in sal and damp riverine forests; summer visitor April — October; confirmed breeding.

ALAUDIDAE
241 Bush Lark *(Mirafra assamica)* 4; in short grassland on dry sand banks along rivers; resident; confirmed breeding.
242 Ashy-crowned Finch Lark *(Eremopterix grisea)* 1; on dry sand banks of the Rapti; resident; possible breeding.
243 Sand Lark *(Calandrella raytal)* 5; along sandy river banks; resident; confirmed breeding.

APODIDAE
244 White-rumped Needletail *(Chaetura sylvatica)* 2; over forests and grasslands; resident?
245 Large White-rumped Swift *(Apus pacificus)* 1; over grasslands near rivers; winter visitor?
246 House Swift *(Apus affinis)* 1; over grasslands and forests; resident? or seasonal visitor.
247 Crested Swift *(Hemiprocne longipennis)* 5; over forests and grasslands; resident; confirmed breeding.
248 Alpine Swift *(Apus melba)* 3; over grasslands and forests; resident?; possible breeding.
249 White-vented Needletail *(Chaetura cochinchinensis)* 1; over rivers; resident?; possible breeding.
250 White-throated Needletail *(Chaetura cauducuta)* 1; over rivers and grasslands; passage migrant.

HIRUNDINIDAE
251 Sand Martin *(Riparia paludicola)* 6; over and along rivers; resident; confirmed breeding.
252 Barn Swallow *(Hirundo rustica)* 4; over open country; resident?; possible breeding.
253 Striated Swallow *(Hirundo daurica)* 4; over open country; resident?; possible breeding.
254 Nepal House Martin *(Delichon nipalensis)* 1; over rivers and forests; winter visitor.

LANIIDAE
255 Bay-backed Shrike *(Lanius vittatus)* 1; recorded by N. Redman & C. Murphy in May 1979; in open forests and grasslands; vagrant.
256 Black-headed Shrike *(Lanius schach)* 3; in grasslands and occasionally in riverine forests; resident; confirmed breeding.
257 Grey-backed Shrike *(Lanius tephronotus)* 1; in scrub forest; winter vagrant.
258 Brown Shrike *(Lanius cristatus)* 1; in grassland/riverine forest; winter visitor September — April.

ORIOLIDAE
259 Golden Oriole *(Oriolus oriolus)* 5; in riverine and sal forests; summer visitor March — October; possible breeding.
260 Black-naped Oriole *(Oriolus chinensis)* 1; in sal and riverine forests; winter visitor?
261 Black-headed Oriole *(Oriolus xanthornus)* 6; in sal and riverine forests; resident; confirmed breeding.
262 Maroon Oriole *(Oriolus traillii)* 1; recorded by H. Tyabji November 1981; in sal forest; winter vagrant.

DICRURIDAE
263 White-bellied Drongo *(Dicrurus caerulescens)* 4; in sal and riverine forests; resident? possible breeding.
264 Small Racquet-tailed Drongo *(Dicrurus remifer)* 3; in sal forest; resident? or winter visitor.
265 Large Racquet-tailed Drongo *(Dicrurus paradiseus)* 3; in sal forest; resident; confirmed breeding.

266 Hair-crested Drongo *(Dicrurus hottentottus)* 4; in sal and riverine forests; resident; possible breeding.
267 Ashy Drongo *(Dicrurus leucophaeus)* 4; in sal and riverine forests; resident? or summer visitor; confirmed breeding.
268 Black Drongo *(Dicrurus adsimilis)* 4; in riverine forest/grassland and open, monotypic sal forest; resident; possible breeding.
269 Little Bronzed Drongo *(Dicrurus aeneus)* 5; in sal and riverine forests; resident; confirmed breeding.
270 Crow-billed Drongo *(Dicrurus annectans)* 5; in sal and riverine forests and grasslands; resident; possible breeding.

ARTAMIDAE
271 Ashy Wood-Swallow *(Artamus fuscus)* 4; in sal and riverine forests; resident; confirmed breeding.

STURNIDAE
272 Spot-winged Stare *(Saraglossa spiloptera)* 4; in riverine forest; spring visitor February — April in large numbers, also seen in July; passage migrant.
273 Brahminy Myna *(Sturnus pagodarum)* 1; only a few sight records in spring; in riverine forest; resident?
274 Grey-headed Myna *(Sturnus malabaricus)* 4; in riverine and sal forests; resident? or summer visitor February — October; confirmed breeding.
275 Eurasian Starling *(Sturnus vulgaris)* 1; in open areas near park's edge; passage migrant (late October 1981).
276 Pied Myna *(Sturnus contra)*

3; along the Rapti near cattle and buffalo; resident; confirmed breeding.
277 Common Myna *(Acridotheres tristis)* 3; in riverine forest/grassland and along rivers; occasionally in sal forest; resident; confirmed breeding.
278 Bank Myna *(Acridotheres ginginianus)* 3-4; in open areas along rivers, especially the Rapti; resident; confirmed breeding.
279 Jungle Myna *(Acridotheres fuscus)* 6; in sal/riverine forests, grasslands and along rivers; resident; confirmed breeding.
280 Talking Myna *(Gracula religiosa)* 3-4; in sal and riverine forests; resident; confirmed breeding.

CORVIDAE
281 Green Magpie *(Cissa chinensis)* 2; in sal forest and also in riverine forest; resident; possible breeding.
282 Red-billed Blue Magpie *(Cissa erythrorhyncha)* 3; in sal forest; resident; possible breeding.
283 Indian Tree Pie *(Dendrocitta vagabunda)* 4; in riverine and sal forests; resident; confirmed breeding.
284 Jungle Crow *(Corvus macrorhynchos)* 5; in sal and riverine forests; resident; confirmed breeding.
285 House Crow *(Corvus splendens)* 1; at park's edge near settlements; resident (outside park); confirmed breeding (outside park).

CAMPEPHAGIDAE
286 Lesser Wood-Shrike *(Tephrodornis pondicerianus)* 4; in sal and riverine forests; resident; confirmed breeding.
287 Large Wood-Shrike *(Tephrodornis gularis)* 4; in sal

and riverine forests; resident; possible breeding.
288 Pied Wood-Shrike *(Hemipus picatus)* 5; in sal and riverine forests; resident; possible breeding.
289 Large Cuckoo-Shrike *(Coracina novaehollandiae)* 5; in sal and riverine forests; resident; possible breeding.
290 Dark Cuckoo-Shrike *(Coracina melaschistos)* 2-3; in riverine forest and sal forest; resident?; possible breeding.
291 Long-tailed Minivet *(Pericrocotus ethologus)* 2; in riverine and sal forests; winter visitor October — April.
292 Scarlet Minivet *(Pericrocotus flammeus)* 5; in sal and riverine forests; resident; confirmed breeding.
293 Rosy Minivet *(Pericrocotus roseus)* 4; in sal and riverine forests; resident? or summer visitor; possible breeding.
294 Small Minivet *(Pericrocotus cinnamomeus)* 3; in sal and riverine forests; resident; confirmed breeding.

IRENIDAE
295 Iora *(Aegithina tiphia)* 5; in sal and riverine forests; resident; confirmed breeding.
296 Golden-fronted Leaf Bird *(Chloropsis aurifrons)* 4; in sal and riverine forests; resident; confirmed breeding
297 Orange-bellied Leaf Bird *(Chloropsis hardwickii)* 2; in sal and riverine forests; resident; possible breeding.

PYCNONOTIDAE
298 Black-headed Yellow Bulbul *(Pycnonotus melanicterus)* 3-4; in sal and riverine forests; resident; confirmed breeding.
299 Red-whiskered Bulbul *(Pycnonotus jocosus)* 6; in sal

and riverine forests and grasslands; resident; confirmed breeding.
300 White-cheeked Bulbul *(Pycnonotus leucogenys)* 3; in sal and riverine forests; resident; confirmed breeding.
301 Red-Vented Bulbul *(Pycnonotus cafer)* 6; in sal forest and riverine forest/grassland; resident; confirmed breeding.
302 White-throated Bulbul *(Criniger flaveolus)* 1; in sal and riverine forests; vagrant.
303 Grey Bulbul *(Hypsipetes madagascariensis)* 3; in sal and riverine forests; resident; confirmed breeding.

TIMALIIDAE
304 Spotted Babbler *(Pellorneum ruficeps)* 5; in sal and riverine forests; resident; confirmed breeding.
305 Slaty-headed Scimitar Babbler *(Pomatorhinus schisticeps)* 3; in sal and riverine forests; resident; confirmed breeding.
306 Rusty-cheeked Scimitar Babbler *(Pomatorhinus erythrogenys)* 2; in sal and riverine forests; resident; possible breeding.
307 Lesser Scaly-breasted Wren Babbler *(Pnoepyga pusilla)* 1-2; in sal and riverine forests near wet gulleys; winter visitor? October — April.
308 Yellow-breasted Babbler *(Macronous gularis)* 5; in sal and riverine forests; resident; confirmed breeding.
309 Black-chinned Babbler *(Stachyris pyrrhops)* 5; in sal and riverine forests; resident; numbers increase in winter; confirmed breeding.
310 Black-throated Babbler *(Stachyris nigriceps)* 4; in sal and riverine forests; resident;

numbers increase in winter; confirmed breeding.
311 Rufous-bellied Babbler *(Dumetia hyperythra)* 1; at edge of sal forest; resident?; possible breeding.
312 Yellow-eyed Babbler *(Chrysomma sinensis)* 4; in riverine forests/grasslands; resident; possible breeding.
313 Red-capped Babbler *(Timalia pileata)* 5; in riverine forests/grasslands and sal/grasslands; resident; confirmed breeding.
314 Jungle Babbler *(Turdoides striatus)* 4; in sal/grasslands and riverine forests/grasslands; resident; possible breeding.
315 Striated Babbler *(Turdoides earlei)* 5; in tall grasslands; resident; confirmed breeding.
316 Slender-billed Babbler *(Turdoides longirostris)* 3; in tall grassland; resident; possible breeding.
317 Lesser Necklaced Laughing Thrush *(Garrulax moniligerus)* 3; in sal and riverine forests; resident; possible breeding.
318 Large Necklaced Laughing Thrush *(Garrulax pectoralis)* 4; in sal forest; resident; possible breeding.
319 Rufous-necked Laughing Thrush *(Garrulax ruficollis)* 4; in riverine forest/grassland and edge of sal forest; resident; confirmed breeding.
320 White-bellied Yuhina *(Yuhina zantholeuca)* 4; in sal and riverine forests; resident?; possible breeding.
321 Nepal Babbler *(alcippe nipalensis)* 2; in sal and riverine forests; resident?

MUSCICAPIDAE
322 Sooty Flycatcher *(Muscicapa sibirica)* 1-2; in sal and riverine forests; seen in

September/October; passage migrant.
323 Brown Flycatcher *(Muscicapa latirostris)* 1; in riverine forests/grasslands; winter visitor; passage migrant.
324 Rufous-tailed Flycatcher *(Muscicapa ruficauda)* 1; in sal and riverine forests; passage migrant (seen in September/October and again in April).
325 Red-breasted Flycatcher *(Muscicapa parva)* 3; in sal and riverine forests; winter visitor September — April.
326 Orange-gorgetted Flycatcher *(Muscicapa strophiata)* 1; in riverine forest; winter visitor October — March.
327 Little Pied Flycatcher *(Muscicapa westermanni)* 2; in sal and riverine forests; winter visitor October — April.
328 Slaty Blue Flycatcher *(Muscicapa leucomelanura)* 1; in riverine forest/grassland and edge of sal forest; winter visitor September — March.
329 Rufous-breasted Blue Flycatcher *(Muscicapa hyperythra)* 1; in sal and riverine forests; winter visitor September — April.
330 Rusty-breasted Blue Flycatcher *(Muscicapa hodgsonii)* 1; in sal and riverine forests; winter visitor October — April.
331 Blue-throated Flycatcher *(Muscicapa rubeculoides)* 1; in sal and riverine forests; winter visitor September — April.
332 Verditer Flycatcher *(Muscicapa thalassina)* 2; in sal and riverine forests; winter visitor September — April/passage migrant.
333 Black-naped Flycatcher *(Monarcha azurea)* 3; in sal and riverine forests; resident? or

summer visitor April — October; confirmed breeding.

334 Brook's Flycatcher *(Muscicapa poliogenys)* 5; in sal and riverine forests; resident; confirmed breeding.

335 Paradise Flycatcher *(Terpisphone paradisi)* 5; in sal and riverine forests; summer visitor March — October; confirmed breeding.

336 White-throated Fantail Flycatcher *(Rhipidura albicollis)* 5; in sal and riverine forests; resident; confirmed breeding.

337 White-breasted Fantail Flycatcher *(Rhipidura aureola)* 3; in sal and riverine forests; resident; possible breeding.

338 Grey-headed Flycatcher *(Culicicapa ceylonensis)* 4; in sal and riverine forests; resident; confirmed breeding.

SYLVIIDAE

339 Slaty-bellied Ground Warbler *(Tesia cyaniventer)* 1; prefers moist spots in sal and riverine forests; winter visitor October — March.

340 Chestnut-headed Ground Warbler *(Tesia castaneo-coronata)* 1; prefers moist spots in riverine and sal forests; winter visitor October — March.

341 Blanford's Bush Warbler *(Cettia pallidipes)* 3-4; where sal intergrades with grass; resident; possible breeding.

342 Aberrant Bush Warbler *(Cettia flavolivaceus)* 1; in riverine forest/grassland and edge of sal forest; winter visitor October — April.

343 Large Bush Warbler *(Cettia major)* 1; in grassland; winter visitor October — April.

344 Rufous-capped Bush Warbler *(Cettia brunnifrons)* 2; in grasslands; winter visitor October — April.

345 Golden-headed Cisticola *(Cisticola exilis)* 2; in tall grassland; resident; possible breeding.

346 Zitting Cisticola *(Cisticola juncidis)* 3; in grasslands; resident?; possible breeding.

347 Hodgson's Prinia *(Prinia hodgsonii)* 4; in sal and riverine forests/grasslands; resident; confirmed breeding.

348 Grey-capped Prinia *(Prinia cinereocapilla)* 4; in sal and riverine forests/grasslands; resident; confirmed breeding.

349 Jungle Prinia *(Prinia sylvatica)* 3; in sal and riverine forests/grasslands; resident; possible breeding.

350 Plain Prinia *(prinia subflava)* 2; in grasslands and sal/grasslands; resident; possible breeding.

351 Ashy Prinia *(Prinia socialis)* 3; in grassland especially where it intergrades with sal and riverine forests; resident; possible breeding.

352 Yellow-bellied Prinia *(Prinia flaviventris)* 4; in grasslands; resident; confirmed breeding.

353 Fulvous-streaked Prinia *(Prinia gracilis)* 1; in grasslands; resident?; possible breeding.

354 Brown Hill Prinia *(Prinia criniger)* 2; on grassy ridges of the Siwalik Hills; resident? or winter visitor.

355 Large Grass Warbler *(Graminicola bengalensis)* 3; in tall grassland; resident; possible breeding.

356 Tailor Bird *(Orthotomus sutorius)* 5; in sal and riverine forests; resident; confirmed breeding.

357 Striated Marsh Warbler *(Megalurus palustris)* 1; in wet grasslands; resident; possible breeding.

358 Great Reed Warbler

(Acrocephalus stentoreus) 1-2; in swampy grasslands; winter visitor October — April.

359 Blyth's Reed Warbler *(Acrocephalus dumetorum)* 3; in riverine forests/grasslands; winter visitor?/passage migrant.

360 Paddyfield Warbler *(Acrocephalus agricola)* 1-2; in tall, wet grasslands; winter visitor September — April.

361 Lesser Whitethroat *(Sylvia curruca)* 1; recorded in scrub forest; winter visitor?

362 Brown Leaf Warbler *(Phylloscopus collybita)* 4; in riverine and sal forests; winter visitor October — April.

363 Tickell's Leaf Warbler *(Phylloscopus affinis)* 2; in riverine and sal forests; winter visitor October — April.

364 Smoky Leaf Warbler *(Phylloscopus fuligiventer)* 1; in riverine forest/grasslands; winter visitor?/passage migrant.

365 Dusky Leaf Warbler *(Phylloscopus fuscatus)* 1; in riverine forest/grassland; winter visitor?/passage migrant.

366 Dull Leaf Warbler *(Phylloscopus trochiloides)* 4; in sal and riverine forests; winter visitor October — March.

367 Large-billed Leaf Warbler *(Phylloscopus magnirostris)* 1; in riverine forest; winter visitor October — April/passage migrant.

368 Plain Leaf Warbler *(Phylloscopus inornatus)* 3; in riverine and edge of sal forests; winter visitor October — March.

369 Yellow-rumped Leaf Warbler *(Phylloscopus proregulus)* 3; in riverine and sal forests; winter visitor October — March.

370 Crowned Leaf Warbler *(Phylloscopus reguloides)* 5; in riverine and sal forests; winter

visitor October — April.
371 Large Crowned Leaf
Warbler *(Phylloscopus
occipitalis)* 5; in riverine and sal
forests; winter visitor
October — April.
372 Yellow-eyed Warbler
(Seicercus burkii) 4; in sal and
riverine forests; winter visitor
October — April.
373 Grey-headed Warbler
(Seicercus xanthoschistos) 3; in
sal and riverine forests; winter
visitor October — April.
374 Chestnut-crowned Warbler
(Seicercus poligenys) 2; in sal
and riverine forests; winter
visitor October — April.
375 Yellow-bellied Warbler
(Abroscopus superciliaris) 2; in
sal and riverine forests; winter
visitor? October — April.

TURDIDAE
376 White-browed Shortwing
(Brachypteryx montana) 1;
recorded in riverine forest by
Dr J. M. Thiollay in
October/November 1978;
winter visitor?
377 Himalayan Rubythroat
(Erithacus pectoralis) 1; in tall,
wet grasslands and at edge of
sal/riverine forests; winter
visitor October — March.
378 Eurasian Rubythroat
(Erithacus calliope) 1; in moist,
tall grassland/riverine forest;
winter visitor October — April.
379 Bluethroat *(Erithacus
svecicus)* 3; in wet, tall
grassland; winter visitor
October — April.
380 Blue Chat *(Erithacus
brunneus)* 1; sal/riverine forest
floor; passage migrant.
381 Shama *(Copsychus
malabaricus)* 5; in dense sal and
riverine forests; resident;
confirmed breeding.
382 Robin Dayal *(Copsychus
saularis)* 5; in sal and riverine

forests; summer visitor March
— October; confirmed breeding.
383 White-tailed Blue Robin
(Cinclidium leucurum) 1; along
headwaters of deep sal forest
streams; winter visitor?
384 Black Redstart
(Phoenicurus ochruros) 3; in
grasslands and near dry river
beds; winter visitor September
— April.
385 White-capped River Chat
(Chaimarrornis leucocephalus)
1; along rivers and forest
streams; winter visitor
November — March.
386 Plumbeous Redstart
(Rhyacornis fuliginosus) 2; on
river banks; winter visitor
September — April.
387 Black-beaked Forktail
(Enicurus immaculatus) 4;
along sal forest streams;
resident; confirmed breeding.
388 Collared Bush Chat
(Saxicola torquata) 5; in
grasslands; resident; possible
breeding.
389 White-tailed Bush Chat
(Saxicola leucura) 4; in
grasslands; resident; confirmed
breeding.
390 Dark-grey Bush Chat
(Saxicola ferrea) 1-2; in
grasslands; winter visitor?
November — March.
391 Pied Bush Chat *(Saxicola
caprata)* 5; in grasslands;
resident; confirmed breeding.
392 Blue Rock Thrush
(Monticola solitarius) 2; along
rivers; winter visitor September
— March.
393 Desert Wheatear *(Oenanthe
deserti)* 1; sight record in April
1981; on dry sandy river beds;
passage migrant? or vagrant.
394 Indian Robin *(Saxicoloides
fulicata)* 1-2; in riverine-forested
open country along park's edge;
resident; possible breeding.
395 Orange-headed Ground

Thrush *(Zoothera citrina)* 5; in
sal and riverine forests; summer
visitor, April — October;
confirmed breeding.
396 Speckled Mountain Thrush
(Zoothera dauma) 1; in sal and
riverine forests near streams;
winter visitor October —
March.
397 Large long-billed Thrush
(Zoothera monticola) 1; sal
forest floor near stream beds;
winter visitor.
398 Grey-winged Blackbird
(Turdus boulboul) 2; in sal and
riverine forests; winter visitor
November — March.
399 Tickell's Thrush *(Turdus
unicolor)* 1; in sal and riverine
forests; winter visitor
?/passage migrant
October/November and April.
400 Black-throated Thrush
(Turdus ruficollis) 5; in riverine
forest; spring visitor February
— April; recorded by
Dr Thiollay in
October/November 1978;
passage migrant?
401 Whistling Thrush
(Myiophoneus caeruleus) 3;
along sal forest streams;
resident; confirmed breeding.

PARIDAE
402 Grey Tit *(Parus major)* 5;
in sal and riverine forests;
resident; confirmed breeding

SITTIDAE
403 Chestnut-bellied Nuthatch
(Sitta castanea) 5; in sal and
riverine forests; resident;
confirmed breeding.
404 Velvet-fronted Nuthatch
(Sitta frontalis) 5; in sal and
riverine forests; resident;
confirmed breeding.
405 Wall Creeper *(Tichodroma
muraria)* 2; on vertical cliffs of
forest streams and rivers; winter
October — March.

MOTACILLIDAE

406 Hodgson's Tree Pipit *(Anthus hodgsoni)* 5; in open sal and riverine forests; winter visitor October — April.
407 Paddyfield Pipit *(Anthus novaeseelandiae)* 5; in open grasslands; resident; confirmed breeding.
408 Richard's Pipit *(Anthus novaeseelandiae richardi)* 2; in grasslands; winter visitor.
409 Rose-breasted Pipit *(Anthus roseatus)* 2-3; on grassy and open river and stream beds; winter visitor October — April/May/passage migrant.
410 Eurasian Tree Pipit *(Anthus trivialis)* 1; in riverine forest/grassland; winter visitor October — March.
411 Forest Wagtail *(Motacilla indica)* 1; sight record by C. Lindahl in 1979; vagrant.
412 Yellow Wagtail *(Motacilla flava)* 4; on moist ground and on grassy river and stream banks; winter visitor September — April.
413 Grey Wagtail *(Motacilla caspica)* 4; along rocky forest streams and stony river beds; winter visitor September — April.
414 Yellow-headed Wagtail *(Motacilla citreola)* 4; on river and stream beds and on moist ground; winter visitor October — April.
415 Pied Wagtail *(Motacilla alba)* 5; along rivers; winter visitor September — April.
416 Large Pied Wagtail *(Motacilla maderaspatensis)* 5; along river banks; resident; confirmed breeding.

DICAEIDAE

417 Thick-billed Flowerpecker *(Dicaeum agile)* 1; in sal forest; winter visitor? October — April.
418 Tickell's Flowerpecker *(Dicaeum erythrorhynchos)* 3; in sal and riverine forests; resident; possible breeding.
419 Fire-breasted Flowerpecker *(Dicaeum ignipectus)* 1; in hill sal forest; winter visitor?

NECTARINIIDAE

420 Scarlet-breasted Sunbird *(Aethopyga siparaja)* 3; in sal and riverine forests; resident; confirmed breeding.
421 Rubycheek *(Anthreptes singalensis)* 1; in sal and riverine forests; resident; possible breeding.
422 Purple Sunbird *(Nectarinia asiatica)* 4; in sal and riverine forests; resident?; confirmed breeding.
423 Little Spiderhunter *(Arachnothera longirostris)* 1; along sal forest streams, partial to wild banana; resident; possible breeding.
424 Streaked Spiderhunter *(Arachnothera magna)* 3; in sal and riverine forests; resident?; possible breeding.

ZOSTEROPIDAE

424 White-eye *(Zosterops palpebrosa)* 6; in sal and riverine forests; resident; confirmed breeding.

PLOCEIDAE

426 House Sparrow *(Passer domesticus)* 3; near human settlements such as Tiger Tops Lodge; disappears during monsoons; confirmed breeding.
427 Yellow-throated Sparrow *(Petronia xanthocollis)* 3; in riverine forest and edge of sal forest; resident?; confirmed breeding.
428 Baya Weaver *(Ploceus philippinus)* 5; in grassland; resident; confirmed breeding.
429 Black-throated Weaver *(Ploceus benghalensis)* 4; in grasslands; resident; confirmed breeding.
430 Red Munia *(Estrilda amandava)* 3; in grasslands; resident; confirmed breeding.
431 Sharp-tailed Munia *(Lonchura striata)* 3; in riverine forest/grassland and at edge of sal forest; resident; possible breeding.
432 Spotted Munia *(Lonchura punctulata)* 5; in sal forest and where it intergrades with grassland; resident; confirmed breeding.
433 Black-headed Munia *(Lonchura malacca)* 4; in tall grassland; resident; confirmed breeding.

FRINGILLIDAE

434 Common Rose Finch *(Carpodacus erythrinus)* 4; in riverine forest; spring visitor February — April; recorded by Dr J. M. Thiollay in October/November 1978; passage migrant.

EMBERIZIDAE

435 Red-headed Bunting *(Emberiza bruniceps)* 1; at edge of park; not recorded in recent years; passage migrant? or vagrant.
436 Yellow-breasted Bunting *(Emberiza aureola)* 3; in grassland and along park's edge; winter visitor November — March/April.
437 Black-faced Bunting *(Emberiza spodocephala)* 1; sighted on 2nd March 1981; in grassland; passage migrant?
438 Grey-headed Bunting *(Emberiza fucata)* 1; in grassland; winter visitor November — March/April.
439 Crested Bunting *(Melophus lathami)* 3; in grasslands and where it intergrades with forests; winter visitor? October — April.

APPENDIX B

Plants and Trees

The following plants and trees were collected by Andrew Laurie in 1978 from inside and outside the park:

ACANTHACEAE
1 *Adhatoda vasica Nees.*
2 *Phlogacanthus thyrsiflorus (Roxb.) Nees.*
3 *Rungia parviflora Nees.*
4 *Goldfussia nutans Nees.*

ANACARDIACEAE
5 *Buchanania latifolia Roxb.*
6 *Lannea coromandelica (Houtt.) Merr.*
7 *Mangifera indica L.*
8 *Rhus javanica L.*
9 *Semecarpus anacardium L.f.*

ANONACEAE
10 *Miliusa velutina H.f. & Th.*

AMARANTACEAE
11 *Alternanthera sessilis (L.) DC.*

APOCYANACEAE
12 *Alstonia scholaris (L.) R. Brown*
13 *Holarrhena antidysentrica Wallich ex DC.*
14 *Vallaris solanaceae (L.) O. Kuntze*

ARACEAE
15 *Pistia stratiotes L.*
16 *Remusatia sp.*

ASCLEPIADACEAE
17 *Calotropis gigantea (L.) Dryand.*

BAMBUSACEAE
18 *Dendrocalamus strictus Nees.*

BIGNONIACEAE
19 *Stereospermum chelonoides (L.f.) DC.*

BIXACAEA
20 *Xylosma longifolium Clos.*

BOMBACACEAE
21 *Bombax ceiba L.*

BORAGINACEAE
22 *Ehretia laevis Rxob.*
23 *Cordia grandis Roxb.*
24 *Cynoglossum zeylanicum Thunberg ex Lehmann*
25 *C. glochidiatum Wallich ex Bentham*
26 *C. bifurcatum L.*

BURSERACEAE
27 *Garuga pinnata Roxb.*

CARYOPHYLLACEAE
28 *Polycarpon indicum (Forsk) Asher & Schweinf.*
29 *Stellaria sp.*

CAPPARIDACEAE
30 *Cleome sp.*

CELASTRACEAE
31 *Cassine glauca (Rottb.) O. Kuntze*

CERATOPHYLLACEAE
32 *Ceratophyllum demersum L.*

CHENOPODIACEAE
33 *Chenopium album L.*

COMBRETACEAE
34 *Anogneissus latifolius (Roxb.) Wall.*
35 *Terminalia bellirica (Gaertr Roxb.*
36 *T. chebula Retz.*
37 *T. Aleta Heyne ex Roth.*

COMPOSITAE
38 *Ageratum conyzoides L.*
39 *Artemisia vulgaris L.*
40 *A. indica Willd.*
41 *Caesulia axillaris Roxb.*
42 *Cirsium wallichii DC.*
43 *Eclipta prostrata L.*
44 *Erigeron bonariensis L.*
45 *Eupatorium odoratum L.*
46 *Gnaphalium luteo-album*
47 *Inula cappa DC.*
48 *Youngia japonica (L.) DC.*
49 *Crassocephalum crepidioid*

COMMELINACEAE
50 *Commelina bengalensis L.*
51 *Commelina sp.*
52 *Cyanotis sp.*

CONIFERAE
53 *Pinus roxburghii Sargent*

CONVOLVULACEAE
54 *Argyreia speciosa Sweet*
55 *A. roxburghii Choisy*
56 *Cuscuta reflexa Roxb.*
57 *Ipomoea quamoclit L.*
58 *I. aquatica Forsk.*

CRUCIFERAE
59 *Rorippa nasturtium-*

aquaticum (L.) Hayek
60 *Raphanus sativus L.*

CUCURBITACEAE
61 *Zehneria maysorensis (Wight. & Arn.) Arn.*
62 *Z. indica (Lour.) Keraudren-Aymonin*
63 *Mukia maderaspatana (L.) Roem.*
64 *Trichosanthes dioica L.*
65 *Cucumis sativus L.*

CUPULIFERAE
66 *Alnus nepalensis D. Don*

CYPERACEAE
67 *Carex continua C.B. Clarke*
68 *Scleria laevis Retz.*
69 *Kyllinga brevifolia Rottboell*
70 *K. colorata (L.) Druce*
71 *Mariscus sieberianus Nees ex Steudl.*
72 *M. paniceus (Rottb.) Vahl*
73 *Cyperus difformis L.*
74 *C. digitatus Roxb.*
75 *C. mersuri L.*
76 *C. niveus L.*
77 *C. pilosus Vahl*
78 *C. rotundus L.*
79 *Fimbristylis dichotoma (L.) Vahl*
80 *Schoeno-plectus mucronatus (L.) Palla*
81 *Pycreus globosus (All.) Reichenb.*

DILLENIACEAE
82 *Dillenia indica L.*
83 *Dillenia pentagyna Roxburgh.*

DIOSCOREACEAE
84 *Dioscorea sp.*

DIPTHEROCARPACEAE
85 *Shorea robusta Gaertn.f.*

ELAEOCARPACEAE
86 *Elaeocarpus tectorius (Lour.) Poir*

EQUISETACEAE
87 *Equisetum sp.*
88 *E. debile Roxb.*

EUPHORBIACEAE
89 *Baccaurea sapida (Roxb.) Muell-Arg.*
90 *Bridelia retusa Spreng.*
91 *Croton grandis Roxb.*
92 *Macaranga denticulata Muell.-Arg.*
93 *Mallotus philippinensis (Lam.) Muell.-Arg.*
94 *M. nepalensis Muell.-Arg.*
95 *Macaranga indica Wight.*
96 *Euphorbia hirta L.*
97 *E. fusiformis Buch.-Ham. ex D. Don*
98 *Phyllanthus emblica L.*
99 *Drypetes roxburghii (Wall.) Hurusawa*
100 *Trewia nudiflora L.*
101 *Sapium insigne Benth.*

FLACOURTICEAE
102 *Casearia glomerata Roxb.*

GENTIANACEAE
103 *Swertia angustifolia Hamilton ex D. Don*

GRAMINAE
104 *Apluda mutica L.*
105 *Aristida adscensionis L.*
106 *Arundo donax L.*
107 *Arundinella bengalensis (Spreng.) Druce*
108 *A. nepalensis Trin.*
109 *Brachiaria ramosa (L.) Stapf.*
110 *Capillipedium assimile (Steud.) A. Camus*
111 *Chrysopogon aciculatus (Retz.) Trin.*
112 *C. gryllus (L.) Trin.*
113 *Coix lachryma-jobi L.*
114 *Cymbopogon flexuosus (Nees ex Steud.) W. Wats*
115 *C. olivieri (Boiss.) Bor*
116 *C. pendulus (Nees ex Steud.)*
117 *Cynodon dactylon (L.) Pers.*

118 *Dactyloctenium aegyptium (L.) P. Beauv.*
119 *Desmostachya bipinnata (L.) Stapf.*
120 *Digitaria ciliaris (Retz.) Koeler*
121 *D. setigera Roth apud Roem et Schult.*
122 *Echinochloa colona (L.) Link*
123 *E. crusgalli (L.) P. Beauv.*
124 *Eleusine indica (L.) Gaertn.*
125 *Eragrostis atrovirens (Desf.) Trin ex Steud.*
126 *E. ciliaris (L.) R. Br.*
127 *E. coarctata Stapf. apud Hook.f.*
128 *E. japonica (Thunb.) Trin.*
129 *E. tenella (L.) P. Beauv. ex Roem et Schult.*
130 *E. unioloides (Retz.) nees ex Steud.*
131 *Hygrorhyza aristata (Retz.) Nees ex Wight & Arn.*
132 *Eulalia fastigiata (Nees) Haines*
133 *Eulaliopsis binata (Retz.) C.E. Hubbard*
134 *Hemarthria compressa (L.f.) R. Br.*
135 *Heteropogon contortus (L.) P. Beauv. ex Roem & Schult.*
136 *Imperata cylindrica (L.) P. Beauv.*
137 *Leptochloa chinensis (L.) Nees*
138 *Narenga fallax (Balansa) Bor*
139 *N. porphyrocoma (Hance) Bov.*
140 *Neyraudia reynaudiana (Kunth) Kent ex Hitchc.*
141 *Oplismenus sp.*
142 *Panicum cambogiense Balansa*
143 *Paspalum distichum L.*
144 *P. scrobiculatum (L.)*
145 *Paspalidium flavidum (Retz.) A. Camus*
146 *Phragmites karka (Retz.) Trin. ex Steud.*
147 *Pogonatherum crinitum (Thunb.) Kunth*

148 *Pseudopogonatherum contortum (Brongy.) A. Camus*
144 *Polypogon monspeliensis (L.) Desf.*
150 *Saccharum arundinaceum Retz.*
151 *S. munja Roxb.*
152 *S. procerum Roxb.*
153 *S. spontaneum L.*
154 *Eranthus filifolius (Steud.) Hackel*
155 *E. longisetosus Anderson*
156 *E. rufipilus (Steud.) Griseb.*
157 *E. ravennae (L.) Beauv.*
158 *Setaria glauca (L.) Beauv.*
159 *S. pallide-fusca (Schumach.) Stapf. & C.E. Hubbard*
160 *S. plicata (Lam.) T. Cooke*
161 *Sporobolus diander (Retz.) P. Beauv.*
162 *Themeda arundinaceae (Roxb.) Ridley*
163 *T. caudata (Nees.) A. Camus*
164 *T. villosa (Poir.) A. Camus*
165 *Thyrsia zea (Clarke) Stapf.*
166 *Thysanolaena maxima (Roxb.) O. Kuntze*
167 *Vetiveria zizanoides (L.) Nash*
168 *Zea mays L.*
169 *Oryza sativa L.*
170 *Triticum arvense L.*

GNETACEAE
171 *Gnetum sp.*

HYDROCHARITIACEAE
172 *Hydrilla verticillata (L.f.) Royle*
173 *Vallisneria natans (Lour.) Hara*

HYPOXIDACEAE
174 *Cucurligo orchioides*

LABIATAE
175 *Colebrookia oppositifolia Smith*
176 *Rabdosia coetsa (Buch.-Ham. ex D. Don) Hara*

177 *Leucas mollissima Wall.*
178 *L. plukenetii Spreng.*
179 *Micromeria integerrimum Benth.*
180 *Pogostemon bengalensis (Burm. f.) O. Kuntze*

LAURACEAE
181 *Litsaea monopetala (Roxb.) Persoon*
182 *Persea sp.*

LECYTHIDACEAE
183 *Careya arborea Roxb.*

LEGUMINOSAE
184 *Acacia catechu (L.f.) Willdenow*
185 *A. pennata (L.) Willdenow Willdenow*
186 *A. concinna DC.*
187 *A. lenticularis Buch.-Ham.*
188 *Albizzia gamblei Prain*
189 *A. lebbek (L.) Benth.*
190 *A. lucinda Bentham*
191 *A. odoyatissima Benth.*
192 *Bauhinia malabarica Roxburgh*
193 *B. purpurea L.*
194 *B. racemosa Lam.*
195 *B. vahlii Wight & Arnott*
196 *B. variegata L.*
197 *Butea monosperma (Lam.) Tanb.*
198 *Cassia fistula L.*
199 *Dalbergia sissoo Roxb.*
200 *D. stipulaceae Roxburgh*
201 *Erythrina suberosa Roxb.*
202 *Millettia extensa (Benth.) Baker*
203 *Flemingia strobilifera (L.) R. Br. ex Ait.*
204 *Desmodium oojeinense (Roxb.) Ohashi*
205 *Spathobolus parviflorus (Roxb.) O. Kuntze*
206 *Crotalaria albida Hyne ex Roth*
207 *Indigophera pulchella Roxburgh*
208 *Trigonella sp.*

209 *Caesalpinia bonduc (L.) Roxb.*
210 *C. decapetala (Roth.) Alston*
211 *Cajanus sativa L.*
212 *Cassia tora L.*
213 *Desmodium sp.*
214 *Lespedeza eriocarpa DC.*
215 *Mimosa rubricaulis Lam.*
216 *M. pudica L.*

LEMNACEAE
217 *Lemna perpusilla Torrey*
218 *Spirodela polyryza L.*
219 *Wolffia globosa (Roxb.) Hartog & Plas*

LENTIBULARIACEAE
220 *Utricularia aurea Loureiro*

LILIACEAE
221 *Asparagus racemosus Willd.*
222 *Smilax lanceifolia Roxb.*
223 *S. ovalifolia (Roxb.) ex D. Don*
224 *Allium cepa L.*
225 *A. sativum L.*
226 *A. wallichii Kunth.*

LINACEAE
227 *Reinwardtia indica Dumortier*

LOGANIACEAE
228 *Buddleia asiatica Lour.*

LYTHRACEAE
229 *Lagerstroemia parviflora Roxb.*
Rotala rotundifolia (Roxb.) Koehne in Engl.
Woodfordia fructicosa (L.) Kurz.

MALVACEAE
230 *Kydia calycina Roxb.*
231 *Hibiscus sp.*
232 *Sida acuta Burman F.*
233 *S. rhombifolia L.*
234 *Thespesia lampas (Cavan.) Dalz et Gibs.*

235 *Urena labota L.*

MARSILIACEAE
236 *Marsilia tetraphylla L.*

MELASTOMACEAE
237 *Osbeckia sp.*
238 *Melastoma melabathricum L.*

MELIACEAE
239 *Azanirachta indica A. Juss*
240 *Toona ciliata M. Roem.*
241 *Chisocheton paniculatus L.*

MENISPERMACEAE
242 *Stephania japonica (Thunb.) Miers*
243 *Holoptelea integrifolia Planch*

MORACEAE
244 *Ficus semicordata Hamilton ex J.E. Smith*
245 *F. glaberrima Bl.*
246 *F. racemosa L.*
247 *F. religiosa L.*
248 *F. auriculata Loureiro*
249 *Cannabis sativa L.*
250 *Streblus asper Loureiro*

MUSACEAE
251 *Musa balbisiana Colla*

MYRTACEAE
252 *Syzygium cumini (L.) Skeels*
253 *S. operculatus (Roxb.) Merr.*
254 *Eucalyptus sp.*
255 *Psidium guajava L.*

OPHIOGLOSSACEAE
256 *Helminthostachys zeylanicus (L.) Hooker*
257 *Ophioglossum petiolatum Hooker*

ORCHIDACEAE
258 *Ponerorchis sp.*

OXALIDACEAE
259 *Oxalis corniculata L.*

PALMAE
260 *Calamus tenuis Roxb.*
261 *Phoenix acaulis Buch.*
262 *P. humilis Royle*

PIPERACEAE
263 *Piper nepalense Miguel*

POLYGALACEAE
264 *Polygala sp.*
265 *P. abyssinica R. Br.*

POLYGONACEAE
266 *Persicaria barbata (L.) Hara*
267 *Polygonum plebujum R. Brown*
268 *Persicaria glabra (Willd.) Hara*

POLYPODIACEAE
269 *Pteris vittata L.*
270 *Dryopteris sp.*

PONTEDERIACEAE
271 *Monochoria hastata (L.) Solms.*

POTAMOGETONACEAE
272 *Potamogeton crispus L.*

PUNICACEAE
273 *Punica granatum L.*

RANUNCULACEAE
274 *Ranunculus scleratus L.*

RHAMNACEAE
275 *Zizyphus mauritinia Lam.*
276 *Z. rugosa Lam.*
277 *Rhamnus nipalensis (Wall.) M. Lawson in Hook.f.*

ROSACEAE
278 *Wendlandia tinctoria (Roxb.) DC.*

RUBIACEAE
279 *Adina cordifolia (Willd. ex Roxb.) Hooker f.*
280 *Anthocephalus cadamba Miguel*

281 *Eriobotrya japonica Lindl.*
282 *Hymenodictoyon excelsum (Roxb.) Wallich*
283 *Mitragyna parviflora Korth.*
284 *Knoxia corymbasa Willd.*
285 *Mussaenda macrophylla Wall.*
286 *Hedyotis lineata (Roxb.)*
287 *Coffea bengalensis Heyne ex Roem. & Schultes*
288 *Mussaenda frondosa L.*
289 *Xeromphis spinosa (Thunb.) Keay*

RUTACEAE
290 *Aegle marmelos (L.) Correa*
291 *Citrus medica L.*
292 *Murraya koenigii Spreng.*
293 *Micromelum pubescens Hook.f.*

SABIACEAE
294 *Meliosma simplicifolia (Roxb.) Walpers*

SAPINDACEAE
295 *Nephelium litchi Camb.*

SAPOTACEAE
296 *Aesandra butyraceae (Roxb.)*
297 *Madhuca longifolia (Koeniq) MacBride*

SAURAUIACEAE
298 *Saurauia nepaulensis DC.*

SCHIZAECEAE
299 *Lygodium flexuosum (L.) SW*
300 *L. japonicum (Thunb.) SW*

SCITAMINAE
301 *Zingiber capitatum Roxb.*
302 *Hedychium spicatum Smith in Rees*
303 *Globba racemosa Smith*
304 *Zingiber officinale Rosc.*

SCROPHULARIACEAE
305 *Scoparia dulcis L.*

SELAGINELLACEAE
306 *Selaginella fulcrata*

SIMARUBACEAE
307 *Brucea mollis Wall.*

SOLANACEAE
308 *Solanum indicum L.*
309 *S. erianthum D. Don*
310 *S. torvum Swartz.*
311 *S. surabtense Burm.f.*
312 *Nicotiana tabacum L.*
313 *Datura sp.*
314 *Capsicum annum L.*

SONNERATIACEAE
315 *Duabanga grandiflora*
(Roxb.) Walpers

STAPHYLACEAE
316 *Bischofia javanica Blume*

STERCULIACEAE

317 *Sterculia pallens Wall.*
318 *S. villosa Roxb.*

TAMARICACEAE
319 *Tamarix dioica Roxb.*
320 *T. indica Willd.*

TETRAMELACEAE
321 *Tetrameles nudiflora R. Br.*

THEACEAE
322 *Schima wallichii (DC.)*
Korthals

TILLIACEAE
323 *Grewia subinaequalis DC.*
324 *G. hainesiana Hole*
325 *G. pumila Buch.-Ham.*
326 *G. sclerophylla Roxb.*
327 *Triumfetta sp.*

TYPHACEAE
328 *Typha elephantina Roxb.*

UMBELLIFERAE
329 *Oenanthe javanica (Bl.)*
DC.
330 *Selinum tenuifolium Wall*
ex C.B. Clarke var. stolonifera
(DC.) Murata

URTICACEAE
331 *Gonostegia pentandra*
(Roxb.) Mig.
332 *Boehmeria macrophylla*
D. Don
333 *Urtica dioica L.*

334 *Girardinia diversifolia*
(Link) Frils et al (ined.)

VERBENACEAE
335 *Gmelina arborea L.*
356 *Tactona grandis L.*
337 *Caryopteris odorata*
(D. Don) B.L. Robinson
338 *Verbena officinalis L.*
339 *Callicarpa macrophylla*
Vahl.
340 *Clerodendron viscosum*
Ventenat
341 *Lantana camara L.*
342 *Premna obtusifolia R. Br.*
343 *Lippia nudiflora Rich*

VITACEAE
344 *Leea compactiflora Kurz.*
345 *L. indica (Burm.f.) Merr.*

Sources: Brandis (1906),
Kanjilal (1911), Bor (1960),
Hara *et al.* (1978).

APPENDIX C

Butterflies

AMATHUSIIDAE
1 Common Duffer *Discophora sondaica*

DANAIDAE
2 Plain Tiger *Danaus chrysippus*
3 Common Tiger *Danaus genutia*
4 Blue Glassy Tiger *Danaus limniace*
5 Glassy Tiger *Danaus aglea*
6 Chocolate Tiger *Danaus melaneus*
7 Striped Blue Crow *Euploea mulciber*
8 Common Indian Crow *Euploea core*

HESPERIIDAE
9 Dusky Yellow-breasted Flat *Daimio phisara*
10 Indian Skipper *Spialia galba*
11 Restricted Demon *Notocrypta curvifascia*
12 Grass Demon *Udaspes folus*
13 Palm Red-eye *Erionata thrax*
14 Common Grass Dart *Taractrocera maevius*
15 Indian Dart *Potanthus pseudomaesa*
16 Contiguous Swift *Pelopidas sinensis*
17 Small Branded Swift *Pelopidas matthias*

LYCAENIDAE
18 Common Gem *Poritia hewitsoni*
19 Apefly *Spalgis epius*
20 Silverstreak Blue *Iraota timoleon*
21 Indian Oakblue *Arhopala atrax*
22 Large Oakblue *Arhopala amantes*
23 Centaur Oakblue *Arhopala centaurus*
24 Common Acacia Blue *Surendra vivarna*
25 Yamfly *Loxura atymnus*
26 Common Onyx *Horaga onyx*
27 Common Flash *Rapala pheritima*
28 Slate Flash *Rapala manea*
29 Common Silverlines *Spindasis vulcanus*
30 Angled Sunbeam *Curetis acuta*
31 Indian Sunbeam *Curetis thetis*
32 Common Lineblue *Prosotas nora*
33 Peablue *Lampides boeticus*
34 Common Cerulean *Jamides celeno*

35 Common Pierrot *Castalius rosimon*
36 Gram Blue *Euchrysops cnejus*
37 Pale Grass Blue *Zizeeria maha*
38 Dark Grass Blue *Zizeeria karsandra*
39 Plum Judy *Abisara echerius*
40 Punchinello *Zemeros flegyas*

NYMPHALIDAE
41 Indian Fritillary *Argyreus hyperbius*
42 Common Leopard *Phalanta phalantha*
43 Vagrant *Vagrens egista*
44 Indian Red Admiral *Vanessa indica*
45 Painted Lady *Vanessa cardui*
46 Indian Tortoiseshell *Aglais cashmirensis*
47 Yellow Pansy *Precis hierta*
48 Blue Pansy *Precis orithya*
49 Lemon Pansy *Precis lemonias*
30 Grey Pansy *Precis atlites*
51 Chocolate Pansy *Precis iphita*
52 Danaid Eggfly *Hypolimnas misippus*
53 Great Eggfly *Hypolimnas bolina*
54 Orange Oakleaf *Kallima inachus*
55 Commander *Limenitis procris*
56 Common Sergeant *Athyma perius*
57 Colour Sergeant *Athyma nefte*
58 Common Lascar *Pantoporia hordonia*
59 Common Sailor *Neptis hylas*
60 Common Earl *Tanaecia julii*
61 Grey Count *Tanaecia lepidea*
62 Common Map *Cyrestis thyodamas*
63 Tawny Rajah *Charaxes polyxena*
64 Red Lacewing *Centhosia biblis*
65 Tabby *Pseudergolis wedah*

PAPILIONIDAE
66 Common Bluebottle *Graphium sarpedon*
67 Common Jay *Graphium doson*
68 Tailed Jay *Graphium agamemnon*
69 Spot Swordtail *Graphium nomius*
70 Common Mime *Papilio clytia*

71 Common Mormom *Papilio polytes*
72 Red Helen *Papilio helenus*
73 Great Mormon *Papilio memnon*
74 Lime Swallowtail *Papilio demoleus*
75 Paris Peacock *Papilio paris*
76 Common Rose *Pachliopta aristolochiae*
77 Common Birdwing *Troides helena*

PIERIDAE
78 Large Cabbage White *Pieris brassicae*
79 Yellow Orange Tip *Ixias pyrene*
80 Red-breasted Jezebel *Delias thysbe*
81 Painted Jezebel *Delias hyparete*
82 Common Jezebel *Delias eucharis*
83 Psyche *Leptosia nina*
84 Great Orange Tip *Hebomoia glaucippe*
85 Common Wanderer *Valeria valeria*

86 Common Emigrant *Catopsilia crocale*
87 Lemon Emigrant *Catopsilia pomona*
88 Mottled Emigrant *Catopsilia pyranthe*
89 Common Grass Yellow *Terias hecabe*
90 Three-spot Grass Yellow *Terias blande*
91 Small Grass Yellow *Terias brigitta*

SATYRIDAE
92 Common Evening Brown *Melanitis leda*
93 Bamboo Treebrown *Lethe europa*
94 Treebrown *Lethe confusa*
95 Common Palmfly *Elymnias hypermnestra*
96 Common Bushbrown *Mycalesis perseus*
97 Dark-brand Bushbrown *Mycalesis mineus*
98 Jungle Brown *Orsotrioena medus*
99 Common Fouring *Ypthima kasmira*
100 Common Fivering *Ypthima baldus*

APPENDIX D

Fish

The following fish were collected from the Narayani river system during 1980 by members of the Aberdeen University Expedition to Nepal, and described by Sharon McGladdery, Catherine McLean, Fiona Maisels, William Miller and Mark Allison.

CYPRINIFORMES

CYPRINIDAE
1 Coptee/chillia *Aspidoparia morar*
2 Chipwa *Barilius barila*
3 Pocketa/coblee *Barilius barnu*
4 Motea *Barilius bendelisis*
5 Gollara *Barilius bola*
6 Pocketa *Barilius tileo*
7 Gorahini *Chagunius chagunio*
8 Bitti *Chela laubuca*
9 Rawa *Cirrhinus reba*
10 Laharey *Crossocheilus latius*
11 Bitti *Danio devario*
12 Derwee *Esomus danricus*
13 Boudina *Garra gotyla gotyla*
14 Gurdi *Labeo boga*
15 Kursar *Labeo gonius*
16 Tair *Labeo pangusia*
17 Rohu *Labeo rohita*
18 Choona *Osteobrama cotio*
19 Chooree *Oxygaster gora*
20 Titti/potersoti *Psilorhynchus sucatio*
21 Sidra *Puntius conchonius*
22 Sidra *Puntius sarana*
23 Sidra *Punitius sophore*
24 Sidra *Puntius ticto*
25 Derwee *Rasbora daniconius*
26 Coochi asalla

Schizothoraicthys progastus
27 Mahingi/mallingi *Semiplotus semiplotus*
28 Sahar/rotar *Tor putipora*
29 Boral kay/rotrahee/koran; also mahseer *Tor tor*

COBITIDAE
30 Baghee *Botia dario*
31 Goara *Lepidocephalicthys guntea*
32 Masaney goara *Nemachilus beavani*

SILURIDAE
33 Binhar *Amblyceps mangois*
34 Lundra *Ompok bimaculatus*
35 Borari *Wallago attu*

BAGRIDAE
36 Mystus *mystus* Tengana cavasius
37 Mystus *mystus* Tengara vittatus
38 Osteobagrus *mystus* Tengri aor
39 Osteobagrus *mystus* Tengri seenghala

SACCOBRANCHIDAE
40 Singahi *Herpetoneustes fossilis*

SCHILBEIDAE
41 Boysa/boykha *Clupisoma garua*
42 Boysa/boykha/boykhee *Pseudotropius atherinoides*

SISORIDAE
43 Cotahee *Gagata cenia*
44 Cotinga *Glyptothorax cavia*

CLARIDAE
45 Mangur *Clarias batrachus*

CLUPEIFORMES
(NOTOPTERIDAE)
46 Lepsi *Notopterus notopterus*

MASTACEMBELLIFORMES
47 Melangi bam *Mastacembalus armatus*
48 Melangi bam *Mastacembalus pancalus*

PERCIFORMES
49 Pansieri *Badis badis*
50 Chuna *Chanda baculis*
51 Chuna *Chanda nama*
52 Chuna *Chanda ranga*
53 Gunta/bullabulla *Glossogobius giurus*
54 Dokia *Nandus nandus*

OPHIOCEPHALIFORMES
55 Chiply bhoti *Channa gachua*
56 Sauri *Channa marulius*
57 Casri bhoti *Channa punctatus*
58 Bonar sauri *Channa striatus*

SYMBRANCHIFORMES
59 Anhya bam *Amphipnous cuchia*

BELONIFORMES
60 Drongahee *Xenentodon cuncila*

ANGUILLIFORMES
61 Raja bam *Anguilla bengalensis*

TETRODONTIFORMES
62 Phua *Tetraodon cutcutia*

Anguilla bengalensis (No. 61) was collected only from the Kali Gandaki river and *Schizothoraicthys progastus* (No. 26) only from the Trisuli river, while *Crossecheilus latius* (No. 10) and *Glyptothorax cavia* (No. 44) were collected from both, although all these species may occur in the faster flowing sections of the Narayani.

APPENDIX E

The national parks and wildlife reserves of Nepal

His Majesty's Government introduced the system of national parks, wildlife reserves, hunting reserves and strict nature reserves in the Kingdom of Nepal under the National Parks and Wildlife Conservation Project, which was started in 1973 with technical assistance and additional funds from the United Nations Development Programme and the Food and Agriculture Organisation. The Project ended in 1979. Nepal's national parks and reserves may be divided into the following three regions:

A. LOWLAND REGION

1. *Royal Chitwan National Park* — gazetted 1973. Original area 210 sq. miles, extended to 360 sq. miles in 1978-9. Further eastern extension up to Amlekhganj now under study. Endangered species include tiger, wild dog, sloth bear, rhinoceros, gaur, dolphin, pangolin, gharial, mugger, python, peafowl, giant hornbill, Bengal florican.
2. *Royal Shuklaphanta Wildlife Reserve* — gazetted 1976. Original area 60 sq. miles, to be extended to 120 sq. miles. Endangered species include tiger, elephant, swamp deer.
3. *Royal Bardia (Karnali) Wildlife Reserve* — gazetted 1976. Area 132 sq. miles. Endangered species include tiger, elephant, swamp deer, dolphin, gharial, mugger, Bengal florican.
4. *Kosi Tappu Wildlife Reserve* — gazetted 1976. Original area 12 sq. miles, extended to 25 sq. miles. Endangered species include wild water buffalo.

B. HIMALAYAN REGION

5. *Sagarmatha National Park* — gazetted 1976. Area 480 sq. miles. Endangered species include musk deer, red panda, Impeyan pheasant and crimson-horned pheasant.
6. *Langtang National Park* — gazetted 1976. Area 660 sq. miles. Endangered species include red panda, musk deer, Impeyan and crimson-horned pheasants.
7. *Rara National Park* — gazetted 1977. Area 40 sq. miles. Endangered species include red panda, musk deer and Impeyan pheasant.

C. TRANSHIMALAYAN REGION

8. *Shey National Park* — proposal approved. Area 56 sq. miles. Endangered species include snow leopard, musk deer, nayan *(Ovis ammon hodgsoni).*

BIBLIOGRAPHY

ALI, S. (1949) *Indian Hill Birds,* Oxford University Press, Bombay.
(1977) *Field Guide to the Eastern Himalayas,* Oxford University Press, Bombay.

ALI, S. & RIPLEY, S.D. (1968–1974) *Handbook of the Birds of India and Pakistan,* Oxford University Press, Bombay. Vols 1–10.

BARASH, D.P. (1978) *Sociobiology and Behaviour,* Heinemann Educational Books, London.

BERTRAM, B. (1978) *Pride of Lions,* Scribner, New York.

BLATTER, E. & MILLARD W.S. (1977) *Some Beautiful Indian Trees,* Bombay Natural History Society, Bombay. Revised by W. T. Stearn.

BOLTON, M. (1975) *Royal Chitwan National Park, Management Plan 1975–79,* NEP/72/002, Project Working Document No. 2, UN DP/FAO, Kathmandu.
(1976) *Lake Rara National Park, Management Plan 1976–81,* FO NEP/72/002, Project Working Document No. 3, UN DP/FAO, Kathmandu.
(1976) *Royal Karnali Wildlife Reserve, Management Plan 1976–81,* FO NEP/72/002, Project Working Document No. 4, UN DP/FAO, Kathmandu.

BUSTARD, H.R. (1980) 'Clutch Size, Incubation and Hatching Success of Gharial *(Gavialis gangeticus, Gmelin)* Eggs from Narayani River, Nepal, 1976–1978', *Journal of the Bombay Natural History Society,* Vol. 77, No. 1: 100–105.

BUSTARD, H.R. & CHOUDHURY, B.C. (1980) 'Parental Care in the Saltwater Crocodile *(Crocodylus porosus, Schneider)* and Management Implications', *Journal of the Bombay Natural History Society,* Vol. 77, No. 1: 64–69.

CARRINGTON, R. (1958) *Elephants,* Chatto & Windus, London.

CAUGHLEY, G.J. & MISHRA, H.R. (n.d.) *Interim Suggestions on Wildlife in Nepal,* 1. The Rhino Sanctuary (Preliminary Report).

CHAPLIN, R.E. (1977) *Deer,* Blandford Press Ltd., Dorset.

COTT, H.B. (1961), 'Ecology and Economic Status of the Nile Crocodile', Trans. Zool. Soc. London Vol. 29 Pt. 4.

DEORAS, P.J. (1965) *Snakes of India,* National Book Trust, New Delhi.

DOUGLAS-HAMILTON, I. & O. (1975) *Among the Elephants,* Collins and Harvill Press, London.

EISENBERG, J.F., McKAY, G.M., & JAINUDEEN, M.R. (1971) 'Behaviour of the Asiatic Elephant *(Elephas maximus maximus L.)*', Reprinted from *Behaviour* Vol. 38: 193—225.

EISENBERG, J.F. & SEIDENSTICKER, J.C. (1976) 'Ungulates in Southern Asia: A Consideration of Biomass Estimates for Selected Habitats, *Biol. Conserv.* 10: 293—308.

FLEMING, R.L. (SR.), FLEMING, R.L. (JR.) & BANGDEL, L.S. (1976) *Birds of Nepal,* Kathmandu.

GEE, H.P. (1975) *The Wild Life of India,* Collins, London, Second edition.

JAINUDEEN, M.R., EISENBERG, J.F. & TILAKERATNE, N. (1971) 'Oestrous Cycle of the Asiatic Elephant, *Elephas maximus,* in Captivity', *Journal of Reproduction and Fertility 27;* 321—328.

JAINUDEEN, M.R., McKAY, G.M. & EISENBERG, J.F. 'Observation on Musth in the Domesticated Asiatic Elephant *(Elephas maximus)*', *Mammalia* 247—261.

LAURIE, A. (1978) 'Ecology and Behaviour of the Greater One-horned Rhinoceros *(Rhinoceros unicornis)',* PhD Thesis, University of Cambridge, England.

LAURIE, A. & SEIDENSTICKER, J. (1977) 'Behavioural Ecology of the Sloth Bear *(Melursus ursinus)*', Reprinted from *Journal of Zoology,* London, 182: 187—204.

LEKAGUL, B. & McNEELY, J. (1977) *Mammals of Thailand.* Association for the Conservation of Wildlife, Bangkok. 758pp.

MARTIN, E.B. (1981) 'The Conspicuous Consumption of Rhinos', *Animal Kingdom,* Vol. 84, No. 1: 11—19.

McDOUGAL, C. (1980) *The Face of the Tiger,* André Deutsch, London, Second edition.

McGLADDERY, S., McLEAN, C.A., MAISELS, F.G., MILLER, W.J.L. & ALLISON, M. (1980) 'Aberdeen University Expedition to Nepal 1980', Expedition Report, Kathmandu.

McKAY, G.M. (1973) 'Behaviour and Ecology of the Asiatic Elephant in South-eastern Ceylon', *Smithsonian Contributions to Zoology* No. 125, Smithsonian Institute Press, Washington, DC.

MISHRA, H.R. (1982) 'Ecology of the Chital *(Axis axis)* in Royal Chitwan National Park: With Comparisons with Hog Deer *(Axis porcinus),* Sambar *(Cerrus unicolor)* and Barking Deer *(Muntiacus muntjak)*', PhD dissertation University of Edinburgh.

(1982) 'Balancing Human Needs and Conservation in Nepal's Royal Chitwan Park', *AMBIO* Vol. II No. 5.

MILTON, J.P. & BINNEY, G.A. (1980) 'Ecological Planning in the Nepales Terai: A report on resolving resource conflicts between wildlife conservation and agricultural land use in Padampur Panchayat.' Threshold, International Centre for Environmental Renewal, Washington DC.

MOUNTFORT, G. (1973) *Tigers,* David & Charles Limited, Devon.

(1981) *Saving the Tiger*, The Viking Press, New York and Penguin Books Canada Limited.

OLIVIER, R. (1978) 'Distribution and Status of the Asian Elephant', Oryx, Vol. 14, No. 4: 379—424.

PRATER, S.H. (1971) *The Book of Indian Animals,* Bombay Natural History Society, Bombay. Third edition.

RANGANATHAN, SHANKAR (November 1979), *Agro-Forestry: Employment for Millions.* Tata Press, Bombay.

SCHALLER, G.B. (1967) *The Deer and the Tiger: A study of wildlife in India.* University of Chicago Press.

(1972) *The Serengeti Lion: A study of predator-prey relations.* University of Chicago Press.

SEIDENSTICKER, J. (1976) 'Ungulate Populations in Chitwan Valley, Nepal', *Biol. Conserv.* 10: 183—210.

(1976) 'On the Ecological Separation between Tigers and Leopards,' *Biotropica* 8 (4): 225—234.

SIKES, S.K. (1966) 'The African Elephant, *Loxodonta africana:* a field method for the estimation of age', *Journal of Zoology,* London, 150: 279—295.

SMITH, C. (1981) *Field Guide to Nepal's Butterflies.* Tribhuvan University Press, Tribhuvan University, Kathmandu. (Natural History Museum Bulletin N. 2.)

SMYTHIES, E.A. (1942) *Big Game Shooting in Nepal,* Thacker, Spink & Co. Calcutta.

STAINTON, J.D.A. (1974) *Forests of Nepal,* John Murray, London. Reprint.

SUGIYAMA, Y. (1967) 'Social Organization of Hanuman Langurs.' In *Social Communication among Primates,* University of Chicago Press. 221—236.

SUNQUIST, M.E. (1979) 'The movements and activities of tigers *(Panthera tigris tigris)* in Royal Chitwan National Park, Nepal', PhD Thesis, University of Minnesota.

TAMANG, K.M. (1979) 'Population Characteristics of the Tiger and Its Prey'. Unpublished.

THIOLLAY, J.M. (1978) 'Ornithological Study carried out in Royal Chitwan National Park from October 6 to November 6, 1978', a report to National Parks and Wildlife Conservation Office, Kathmandu. Typed.

WHITAKER, R. (1978) *Common Indian Snakes: A Field Guide.* The Macmillan Company of India Limited, Delhi.

WHITAKER, R. & DANIEL, R.C. (1976) 'The status of Asian Crocodilians', *Tigerpaper,* Vol. 5 No. 4: 12—17.

WILLAN, R.S.M. (1965), 'The Chitwan Wildlife Sanctuary in Nepal', *IUCN Bulletin 8,* Morges, Switzerland.

WILLIAMS, J.H. (1950) *Elephant Bill,* Rupert Hart-Davis, London.

WOODHOUSE, L.G.C. (1950) *The Butterfly Fauna of Ceylon,* Government Publication Bureau, Colombo, Second (abridged) edition.